Powerful
People
Are
Powerful
Performers

A  Book

Powerful People
Are
Powerful Performers

Your Daily Guide
To Becoming A
More Power-Driven Person

Peter Biadasz and Richard Possett

A  Book

iUniverse, Inc.
New York Lincoln Shanghai

Powerful People Are Powerful Performers
Your Daily Guide To Becoming A More Power-Driven Person
A "Power Series" Book

iUniverse books may be ordered through booksellers or by contacting:

iUniverse
2021 Pine Lake Road, Suite 100
Lincoln, NE 68512
www.iuniverse.com
1-800-Authors (1-800-288-4677)

The views expressed in this work are solely those of the author and do not necessarily reflect the views of the publisher, and the publisher hereby disclaims any responsibility for them.

ISBN-13: 978-0-595-41844-2 (pbk)
ISBN-13: 978-0-595-86187-3 (ebk)
ISBN-10: 0-595-41844-9 (pbk)
ISBN-10: 0-595-86187-3 (ebk)

Printed in the United States of America

Foreword

By
Marilyn S. Possett, L.C.S.W.
Psychotherapist ~ Outpatient Services
Laureate Psychiatric Clinic and Hospital

રે⊷ ⊷ร

Powerful People Are Powerful Performers ~ *Your Daily Guide To Becoming A More Power-Driven Person* is a book that provides you with a simple method to facilitate positive changes in your life. The book's regimen is a fast and easy, but effective, daily plan of action for enhancing your living-life performance. It offers you a way for more achievement at work, home, and play. It is a system for greater accomplishment in both your personal and professional worlds. It is a process for increased positive interaction with family, friends, and fellow workers. It is a practice that helps you do better, feel better, and be better at living life. In the final analysis, this book helps you do a little *more* each day for a much better and complete living-life experience.

It goes without saying that a powerful performer looks good, feels good, acts good, and does well. The reason is that they do *more*. They perform at a high potential because they recognized their personal strengths and take positive action to make themselves stronger. Powerful performers spend time identifying their individual weaknesses and then proactively modify these debilities for increased fulfillment. Plainly put, they change their personal behavior patterns, their professional habits for a *more* powerful living-life performance.

Not changing anything in life suggests we will simply stay the same. But, in real life, you either advance or you retreat. You really never stay the same. Therefore, you must learn to change to become *more* productive or you fall back. And, going backwards should not be an option. It is not the way to live a high-performing life. For you see, our goal should be to grow until we die. That is how we express our true humanity. That is how we have a full life. That is how we advance to the ultimate. So, how do we progress?

The term *more* explicitly suggests something greater in amount, degree, or number. Thus, to be *more* powerful clearly connotes we must grow. Growth means change. We must do things differently by beginning to establish new high-powered types of activities. We must modify our current behavior and do away with old counterproductive practices. However, change is something that we earthborn do not handle well. The act of changing can be very difficult for us humans.

Human behavior researchers have identified five stages of change. These stages include awareness, consideration, preparation, action, and maintenance. Simply said, we first come to realize that there are more productive ways for living our lives. We see and acknowledge the need for positive change. Next, we decide to take action. We commit ourselves to making the necessary changes to progress, to advance. And finally, we choose to maintain those new behaviors for our long-term personal and professional benefit.

My professional peers think change is facilitated by eating the elephant—all of those unspoken disconcerting behaviors and habits—in the living room one bite at a time. It is called chunking. Basically, this approach says to start with tiny bites and stay with tiny bites. This procedure is very helpful in digesting difficult conduct; one does it one bite at a time. It is a straightforward method toward establishing new productive behaviors. It is similar to baby steps; that is, progressing in small steps.

This book shows you an easy way, the simple actions necessary to learn new behavior patterns and change old counterproductive habits. For behavior, good or bad, is something that you do, some action that you take. And remember, action is the fourth stage of change. Without it, you simply stay the same. No, you really retreat! This book provides, in tiny daily bites, the material and training necessary to change your behaviors and habits in a fast and easy fashion. This process, if adhered to, can make you a more power-driven person.

Definitions

per·form [pər-fôrm']
v. per·formed, per·form·ing, per·forms
v. tr.

1. To begin and carry through to completion; do: Ralphie performed the daily exercise program.

2. To take action in accordance with the requirements of; fulfill: perform one's obligations: Ralphie accomplished his goals for the day.

v. intr.

1. To carry on; function: Ralphie is a person who performs well with a structured system.

2. To fulfill an obligation or requirement; accomplish something as promised or expected.

---

per·for·mance [pər-fôr'məns]
n.

1. The act of performing or the state of being performed.

2. The way in which someone or something functions: Ralphie rated himself with the Score-More Regimen.

3. Something performed; an accomplishment.

Dedications

I dedicate this book to those mentors who have recognized the extremes in my life and have offered wise counsel regarding balance.

~ *Peter Biadasz*

This particular book is dedicated to Dr. David Ajibade, M.D. whose fervent wish is to make the whole world healthier, one person at a time.

~ *Richard Possett*

Acknowledgements

Thank you to my family, my friends and business associates; you add so much to my personal and professional life. Even though I may not always show it, know that my appreciation runs very deep. (Yes, I have said this before but one can never say it enough.)

~ Peter Biadasz

Thanks to my partners, Marilyn and Peter, for prodding my self-discipline along so as to be more power-driven to finish this book on time. Further kudos to them for their exigent clinical and practical input and advice to keep me properly focused on the subject matter at hand.

~ Richard Possett

Why Read This Book?
(If it's to be, it's up to me!)

This book is about behavioral change and self-discipline. It is concerned with behaviors that are small steps toward a big goal. In the end, the larger objective is to become a more power-driven person. The means is your self-discipline. The way is the Score-More Regimen.

This book is about learning new patterns of behavior and modifying old habits. It is concerned with how these characteristics have an influence on your personal performance in all facets of your life. It should help give you a new view toward being a power-driven person, achieving comprehensive success in the process of living.

In the main, health, wealth, and happiness are elements of a chosen lifestyle. That is, a consistent, integrated way of living as exemplified by your particular attitude and actions. Generally, people do what they prefer to do. Changing the old preferences is very difficult. Establishing new behavior patterns takes practice and patience. This book, utilized appropriately, will help cure counterproductive habits and instill a personal neo-culture made up of a more powerful living-life experience. It will provide guidance leading to a well-rounded and more productive life.

Go ahead, eat, drink, and be merry. But, do it, do it right, and do it right now. For us, "doing it" is integrated fitness ("IF") of the mind, body, and spirit. "IF" can eliminate the 'if-onlys' in daily life: if only I made more money, if only I had a better job, if only I weighed less, if only I were motivated to exercise, if only people liked me more, if only I were healthier, if only I read more books, if only I were more self-driven, if only I were goal oriented, and so on and so forth.

If you want to purge the "if-onlys," if you want to be a good living-life performer and even get better, then **Powerful People Are Powerful Performers** ~ *Your Daily Guide To Becoming A More Power-Driven Person* is the book for you. If you would truly like to cleanse the "if-onlys" from your life, then buy and use this book until you wear it out. Because you are the captain of your own fate, this guidebook, used properly, is your polestar to performing more powerfully at home, work, and play. Through discipline, patience, and practice you make the changes for a powerful life.

Success begets success in all you do in life. This is true whether it is business or personal, on-the-job, or at home. It is certainly right on with family, friends, and fellow-workers. It's also valid for health, confidence, money, diet, character, exercise, self-improvement, conscientiousness, and relationships. The keys to complete success are the self-disciplined life, the power-driven person. Without these two characteristics, we have mediocrity at best and failure at worst. It is your choice. If you are or wish to be a power-driven person with self-discipline, achieving success, then buy this book. If not, simply leave it on the bookshelf because discipline and power are cultivated from within oneself. They are not externally driven. In the final analysis, it is totally up to you. We can only help you achieve your goals.

Discipline and change are developed daily habits. They are a couple of big "IFs" in life. They are your conscious conditioning of integrating mind, body, and spirit into a powerful life force. They are the ultimate good behaviors. They are what make people successful. They are what this book is all about. Buy the book and use the material to help develop a personal culture in which you become a more powerful performer in your way of living life. Now, be gone your "if-onlys" with discipline and change.

Powerful People Are Powerful Performers ~ *Your Daily Guide To Becoming A More Power-Driven Person* is a compendium of Daily Success Scorecards. These tally-tickets have been designed over ten (10) years to be a simple daily record of the key result activities in your life. To begin, you establish and monitor personal and professional goals. Once ascertained, these objectives are assigned scoring points to measure and monitor performance. Then, you track and grade yourself on a daily, weekly, and monthly basis. You make the necessary adjustments to meet or exceed your goals. The process is a fast and easy method to monitor your daily behavior and modify it as needed. With the Score-More Regimen, success is one point at a time. Therefore, stay the course. Take it slowly and steadily, and you will become a more power-driven person.

Contents

Preface
(Be Your Own Best Boss)

This book is about power and performance in living life. As we know, there are multiple layers in life as we live it. Our experiences include personal and professional activities. They consist of interactions with our family, friends, and fellow-workers. We engage in life in the home, on-the-job, and at play. Our lives are the compilation of all these activities in our given time, in our given setting. Our life is a performance of the mind, body, and spirit. It is the accumulation and culmination of our deeds and feats, whether right or wrong, good or bad, strong or weak.

Consciously or unconsciously, functional people prefer right, good, and strong. The deficiency in most people for not powerfully grasping life is their inability to put to use their individual life force and energy. For some reason, they are not fully power-driven people. They operate at only minimal levels of individual endowed power.

Everyone is supplied with power, is a source of power. The key is to harness this individual life force and energy. Therefore, we must explore ways and means to discover and employ our power resources. As stewards of our time, talent, and treasure, it is our responsibility to put them to maximum work. **Powerful People Are Powerful Performers** ~ *Your Daily Guide To Becoming A More Power-Driven Person* is the book that can help you discover, harness, and employ your personal and professional resources with maximum power in all facets of your life.

Over the years, we have been introduced to thousands of regimens for better management, diet, exercise, development, and relationships. In its own way, each one has tried to teach us a myriad of "if-onlys." If only we did this or that, we could be this or that. That is, whatever we wanted to be. We would lose weight, look and feel wonderful, be successful, achieve contentment, and have total control of our lives. Some may have worked. Others may have been worthless. Generally, the results have been short term. We start over again next week, next month, or next year. We yo-yo our way through life.

The Score-More Regimen to a power-driven life may be the thing for you. Its methodology has been time-tested for over ten years and thus will work for you with long-lasting results. It works because it changes your fundamental behaviors and not just short-term actions. It makes you a power-driven person through modified simple daily habits.

The Score-More Regimen is based on one very humble but highly important principle and that is **SELF-DISCIPLINE**. The system is focused solely on one source of power, which is the self. The Score-More Regimen speaks to self-management, self-improvement, self-control, self-development, and self-confidence through self-discipline. It is all about you and what you do to achieve a power-driven life. And you are defined by you as yourself.

Let's consider, one-by-one, some of the subjects that we are talking about.

1. For time management, the process is straightforward. It is good planning, ample communications, and self-discipline.

2. In business matters, the operation is forthright. It is about smart work, achieving results, and self-discipline.

3. For weight management, the system is very simple. It is proper diet, adequate exercise, and self-discipline.

4. In your private life, you need to know what truly is important and then act upon that knowledge with self-discipline.

5. For personal and professional development, the scheme is not complicated. It is reading, studying, and self-discipline.

6. In maintaining healthy relationships, it means having patient perseverance, regarded respect, and self-discipline.

7. For human consciousness, it is simple and straightforward. It is your character, confidence, and self-discipline.

As you readily can see, it's all about a state of knowledge, order, and control. For self-discipline is surely the act of controlling oneself or one's desires, actions, and habits. It is a system of obedience with rules of conduct. But, to whom are you obedient? Who rules? YOU RULE! The Score-More Regimen inculcates a simple daily rigor that cultivates your individual habits of action with moderation and excellence. It is your personal and private training guru helping to transform you into a powerful person. It is your daily guide to a power-driven performance in living life.

Introduction

What Do We Mean by Performance?
(Getting powerful results!)

To begin, let's clear up any potential confusion. Life is not about effort. The real world is concerned with results. It is the outcome and not the exertion that is important. It is termed productivity. In short, it means to be more powerful in what we produce. But our outcomes can be positive or they can be negative. Typically, a negative effort will signify a bad or a lesser result. And the opposite is generally true. That is, a powerful effort can regularly generate a greater conclusion. Then what can make the difference? The answer is our performance. Of course, you can always just depend on getting lucky. Are you feeling lucky today?

Performance is the key element in the power equation. Namely, effort plus performance equals results. A powerful performance will commonly equal a positive conclusion. Conversely, a weak performance will most likely produce a half-empty outcome. Therefore, it is bringing the feat (effort) to fruition (performance) that will cause a happening (result) to be powerful. Powerful performers truly know that the harder and smarter they perform, the luckier they get. These individuals fully understand that success comes to those who are high performing each and every day.

Your performance gauge can run the gamut from high to low. Individually, you may be a moderate performer or you may be a high performing person. If it is high, then how can you make it higher? If it is low, or somewhere in between, how can you take your daily performance to an upper level? These are very good questions. Then the answer, please: it's a behavioral issue.

You move along your performance gauge by modifying your personal behavior. You alter your daily performance habits. Please remember the power formula. So, here we are simply speaking about changing habits, modifying behavior. For most people, it is an easy concept, but a difficult endeavor. The training in this book can help you to develop uncomplicated behavior patterns that are easy to perform each and every day. They will produce a more powerful living-life performance for you. They are doable tactics to vanquish the elephant, one tiny bite at a time.

Who Is a Powerful Performer?
(You!)

A powerful performer is someone who gets things done when they need to be done. They do it! They do it right! And they do it right now! Powerful performers are the class president, team captain, chief executive, and community leader. Truthfully, they typically are the nerds of the world. They are the people who seem to have time for improved performance at work, home, and play. They eat right and exercise. They take time in their day for reading, whether it is personal or professional. These types of people pay attention to themselves and their relationships with other people. They generally oversee people, but most importantly, they manage themselves very well. Powerfully performing individuals control their time, actions, and results. They are self-reliant. Powerful performers take charge and responsibility. They don't play the blame game. They are self-confident but not cocky. They are highly self-disciplined. They are self-motivated. Power-driven people don't have "if-onlys." When called upon to do the job, they get results on time. They do this in both their personal and professional worlds. They always perform powerfully. Powerful performers have created a personal culture, a way of living life, of performing at the highest level.

Getting Started
(Now!)

You start with a plan. This means a life plan (see Exhibit I), an annual plan, a plan of the month, and a weekly plan (see Exhibit II). The Daily Success Scorecard is your day planner. You set your goals, determine the strategies, and employ the tactics. If you need help, engage a personal career development coach and/or planning consultant. The next step is to define the new you. To do that, you must come to grips with the now you. What are your current behaviors and habits? What outcomes do they produce related to your life plan? That is, where are you now? After you have identified where you are with the now you, you must then determine what you want to accomplish with the new you.

A good friend of mine, we shall call him Ralphie, asked me to help him change to be a more powerful performer. Ralphie weighed two hundred eighteen pounds, was tired and listless, bored with his life, his job performance was mediocre, and he was spiritually directionless. After speaking with his doctor, we decided that with his five foot, ten inch frame, he would look and feel good at one hundred seventy-five pounds. Together with a certified personal fitness trainer, we established an exercise regimen in which he would jog three to four times each week for four to five miles in forty-five minutes. We categorized his daily work activities between business and bizyness. After a hard analysis, we established that seventy percent of Ralphie's workday needed to be focused on the business of getting business. We defined that productive time to mean four to five effective hours of selling and marketing each and every business day. We established daily goals for planning, relationships, and personal time. The two of us developed objectives for Ralphie that included nutrition, water intake, dietary supplements, good posture, and breathing exercises. With a schematic of his new self, Ralphie set out on his personal journey to reinvent himself through the Score-More Regimen.

About the Quote Sources
(It is good for man to read books of quotations.)

If you want to receive some further rewards from the Score-More Regimen, perform research on the people quoted in the quote of the day box. You are encouraged to learn about their unique lives and special times. Learning how these individuals became power-driven people in their own right can be fascinating, if not educational. If someone happens to be quoted more than once, research the circumstances surrounding the quotation. In the instances of sayings and proverbs, a study into the traditions associated with each aphorism may be instructive. Consider doing the same for the unknown authors. The results of your study and research, if you like, can be noted in the margins. <u>Here we have an important announcement</u>: please understand that in instances in which a quote or text refers to "him," the word "her" can simply be substituted.

And please remember …

"The wisdom of the wise, and the experience of the ages, may be preserved by quotation."

~ Benjamin Disraeli

For we say …

Tell me … I'll forget

Show me … I'll remember

Involve me … I'll comprehend

So, be powerful to be great, to get better!

BECOME A MORE POWER-DRIVEN PERSON

Exhibit I

My

p^3

Journal

Personal Power Performance

Exhibit I-A

My Mission

- ➢ To take charge of me.

- ➢ To always do my best.

- ➢ To be at peace with God.

- ➢ To live the Golden Rule.

- ➢ To maintain a balanced life.

- ➢ To give more than I ever got.

- ➢ To know justice and honesty.

- ➢ To have a positive personality.

- ➢ To perpetually grow until I die.

- ➢ To fulfill the Paramount Virtues.

- ➢ To leave life better than I found it.

- ➢ To pass on a memorable memory.

RWP

- ➢ To acquire serenity, courage and wisdom.

Exhibit I-B

My Promises

- ➢ Maintain good health
- ➢ Establish the business
- ➢ Expand relationships
- ➢ Be materially debt free
- ➢ Erudition before expiration
- ➢ Publish before perishing
- ➢ Don't burden the children

Exhibit I-C

My Economy

- ➢ REML/PPF Niche
- ➢ Read & Study ConED
- ➢ Polish Literary Works
- ➢ Just4ME Opportunity
- ➢ CHEE/Dustees Enterprise

RWP

Exhibit I-D

My Score

WEIGHT MANAGEMENT			
	TARGET	ACTUAL	NOTES
2006			
08/01	173	172	Out-of-State Trip
08/16	173	176	R2PII OK Visit
09/01	173	174	Labor Day
09/16	173	175	College Football
10/01	173	175	4th Quarter 2006
10/16	173		2007 Biz Plan
11/01	173		Halloween 2006
11/16	173		Thanksgiving 2006
12/01	173		Holiday Season
12/16	173		Merry Christmas
01/01	173		Happy New Year

COMMENTS

Note: Weigh 173 on 8/1/06

6/30/06 172 Actual

7/16/06 175 Actual

8/01/06 172 Actual

Exhibit II

PERSONAL ACTION PLAN

for

Richard W. Possett

"Creating My Economy"

September ~ 2006

Exhibit II-A

4-1-1 Action Goal Worksheet

Name: Richard W. Possett/The SAM Firm

My Annual Goals   Year: 2006

Business

❖Work REBA/REMBO
❖Develop PPF Niche
❖Build CHEE/Dustees
❖Establish Just4ME
❖Smart Networking
❖Husband Resources
❖Complete ConED
❖G&A/PATTs/R&D

Personal

❖Mine Cyrus
❖Liquidate Coins*
❖Literary Works
❖Read & Study Stuff
❖MSP "40%" Retire
❖Focus on Opus
❖Weight Management
❖Afford MtreoManor

My Monthly Goals   Month: September

Business

❖REML/PPF Program
  ◉REBA Regimen
  ◉REMBO DMA
  ◉Bepossettive.com
❖Settle TaDoes ($10K)
❖Execute Maple Leaf
❖CHEE/Dustees Ideas
❖Collect MAC $2300
❖Matriculate ConED
❖Advance Just4ME

Personal

❖Integrated Fitness
❖Care for the family
❖Submit Just4Moms
❖Publish Just4Dads
❖Target $20K P&L
❖Track 3PLeaders
❖Folo Goodness Book
❖Bepowerful.net
❖Trail Cyrus matters
❖Offer 3PPerformers

Exhibit II-B

4-1-1 Action Goal Worksheet

Week One
Business
- ◘ Maple Leaf Invest
- ◘ Settle TaDoes
- ◘ Collect MAC $2300
- ◘ Study ConED
- ◘ G & A Stuff

Personal
- ⦿ Edit Just4Moms
- ⦿ Resubmit Just4Dads
- ⦿ Labor Day Weekend
- ⦿ RWP 63rd Birthday

Week Two
Business
- ◘ Maple Leaf Invest
- ◘ REBA/REMBO Plan
- ◘ bepossettive.com
- ◘ Advance Just4ME
- ◘ Study ConED

Personal
- ⦿ Work Moms & Dads
- ⦿ Folo 3PLeaders
- ⦿ Work 3PPerformers
- ⦿ bepowerful.net

Week Three
Business
- ◘ Maple Leaf Invest
- ◘ Advance Just4ME
- ◘ bepossettive.com
- ◘ Study ConED
- ◘ REBA/REMBO Plan

Personal
- ⦿ Track Moms & Dads
- ⦿ Work 3PPerformers
- ⦿ bepowerful.net
- ⦿ Book of Goodness

Week Four
Business
- ◘ Maple Leaf Invest
- ◘ Advance Just4ME
- ◘ bepossettive.com
- ◘ REBA/REMBO Plan
- ◘ Study ConED

Personal
- ⦿ Book of Goodness
- ⦿ Track Moms & Dads
- ⦿ Submit 3PPerformers
- ⦿ bepowerful.net

Exhibit II-C

2007

January
S	M	T	W	T	F	S
	1	2	3	4	5	6
7	8	9	10	11	12	13
14	15	16	17	18	19	20
21	22	23	24	25	26	27
28	29	30	31			

February
S	M	T	W	T	F	S
				1	2	3
4	5	6	7	8	9	10
11	12	13	14	15	16	17
18	19	20	21	22	23	24
25	26	27	28			

March
S	M	T	W	T	F	S
				1	2	3
4	5	6	7	8	9	10
11	12	13	14	15	16	17
18	19	20	21	22	23	24
25	26	27	28	29	30	31

April
S	M	T	W	T	F	S
1	2	3	4	5	6	7
8	9	10	11	12	13	14
15	16	17	18	19	20	21
22	23	24	25	26	27	28
29	30					

May
S	M	T	W	T	F	S
		1	2	3	4	5
6	7	8	9	10	11	12
13	14	15	16	17	18	19
20	21	22	23	24	25	26
27	28	29	30	31		

June
S	M	T	W	T	F	S
					1	2
3	4	5	6	7	8	9
10	11	12	13	14	15	16
17	18	19	20	21	22	23
24	25	26	27	28	29	30

July
S	M	T	W	T	F	S
1	2	3	4	5	6	7
8	9	10	11	12	13	14
15	16	17	18	19	20	21
22	23	24	25	26	27	28
29	30	31				

August
S	M	T	W	T	F	S
			1	2	3	4
5	6	7	8	9	10	11
12	13	14	15	16	17	18
19	20	21	22	23	24	25
26	27	28	29	30	31	

September
S	M	T	W	T	F	S
						1
2	3	4	5	6	7	8
9	10	11	12	13	14	15
16	17	18	19	20	21	22
23	24	25	26	27	28	29
30						

October
S	M	T	W	T	F	S
	1	2	3	4	5	6
7	8	9	10	11	12	13
14	15	16	17	18	19	20
21	22	23	24	25	26	27
28	29	30	31			

November
S	M	T	W	T	F	S
				1	2	3
4	5	6	7	8	9	10
11	12	13	14	15	16	17
18	19	20	21	22	23	24
25	26	27	28	29	30	

December
S	M	T	W	T	F	S
						1
2	3	4	5	6	7	8
9	10	11	12	13	14	15
16	17	18	19	20	21	22
23	24	25	26	27	28	29
30	31					

Instructions
(If you don't know, you are out of control.)

Score-More Regimen

When you score, you do less and more. It's human nature. Typically, when people set goals and become more accountable, they personally perform at much higher levels. They achieve more than if they didn't score. The uniqueness about the Score-More Regimen is that you are the boss. You determine your goals, measurement, and consequences. Thus, YOU RULE! But, this is a thinking man's program for the serious minded person. That is, one who is truly motivated to be a power-performer in life. Remember, your performance is dependant on you, on your self-discipline. For you are defined by you as yourself. The Score-More Regimen is divided into thirteen-week sections. There are four sections to a year. A scorecard, as a way of illustration, may be labeled as week one, day three on January 3, 2006. Please refer to the very top of the Daily Success Scorecard. Also, you may want to review Getting Started in the Introduction before you begin your regimen.

Different Days

Throughout each month, you will have distinct scores for dissimilar days. On a whole day, you should accumulate one hundred points. On working days, when you rest your body and do not physically exercise, you will muster ninety-three points. On holidays, weekends, PTO (personal time off) days, and vacations you can compile between twenty-three and thirty points a day depending on when your exercise is scheduled during those periods. Therefore, your targeted score goal will vary from month to month. For a typical thirty-day month, you might have between two thousand two hundred and two thousand three hundred and fifty in aggregate points. The total points will be influenced by how you have planned a particular month. Differences will also be due to thirty-one day months, those months that have holidays, and on what day the month begins. Look at a calendar and go ahead, add-'em up, set your goals, and gitter-done.

"*Ne fas*" Days

In the days of the Roman Republic and early empire, one or both proconsuls—there were always two—could read the signs (animal entrails, casting bones, the stars, and other symbols) and proclaim *"Ne fas"* in the morning. This meant that there was something wrong with the day, and the Senate could not meet under such inauspicious circumstances lest something terrible happen. The ability to cancel senatorial deliberations at will was obviously abused for political aims. For that reason, the Senate actually decreed by law how many *"Ne fas"* days a proconsul could declare. In the Score-More Regimen, you have no restrictions, except those controlled by your good self-discipline, on how many *"Ne fas"* days you declare from your diet. If you proclaim a *"Ne fas"* day, record a negative twenty-one points as your caloric score. Also, remember it is your personal objective to have good weight management practices. So, watch those *"Ne fas"* days, but please do have some fun and take a break every now and then from your diet.

Bear-Down Days

Some days you eat the bear and on others, the bear eats you. We all have down days. Please don't fret; you can make up some lost points by working on the weekends and PTO days. Isn't it just great! Furthermore, if you happen to miss an exercise period on a particular day, reschedule and make up the lost activity the next day. If you have overeaten, consider eating a little less on the subsequent days. Of course, you can't ingest or regurgitate food, water, and air from a previous day. So track your habits. Be that as it may, the Score-More Regimen is still a flexible program. Use the adjustability feature. Bear down and bend it, but don't break it.

Business Matters ~ *70 points*

It is very important to structure every day around business and not simply bizyness. This is true if you are working or retired. A lot of people stay busy. They think of themselves as being efficient. That is, doing things right. But, they are not very effective, which is doing the right things. They are in the habit of doing the wrong things really well. If so, let's modify your behavior. In business, make sure that your daily plan is centered on where the money makers matter. If retired, focus on continued growth in your life. The locus of our Score-More Regimen will be on business. To start, carefully analyze your working days to determine where you really spend your time. How much of your time is allocated to SAM (sales and marketing) actions? How do you define your money makers? Here is where you spend your prime time. In those instances where you have PATTs (projects, assignments, tasks, and to-does) that are not specifically and directly related to primary business matters, it is simply bizyness. Score yourself accordingly each day and make the necessary modifications to be more productive where money matters. We call it *Pay-Power*. It is your salary, commission, wage, or other compensation that supports you and your family. It is your lifestyle at stake. And, believe me, I've been rich and I've been poor, and rich is much better. So, work on it and make it work!

Nutrition ~ *10 points*

One very important part of good health and effective weight management is diet. In dieting, it is always best to seek advice from your doctor or speak with a professional nutritionist. In our Score-More Regimen, we adhere to a fat-controlled, low-cholesterol diet plan. We use two thousand daily calories as our benchmark to maintain our goal weight. Naturally, this might differ depending on your age, metabolism, and exercise program. Another critical element of a result-oriented diet and healthy life plan is self-discipline. Restraint and control are inherently decisive in the Score-More Regimen. Therefore, you keep track of your daily food intake and score calories, fats, cholesterol, carbohydrates, and proteins. Reference the tally-ticket and then see the illustration for an example. Nutritional facts are recorded on most boxes, containers, and packages of food. Furthermore, you can purchase a book on nutrition for those items that are not measured by the manufacturer and for dining out in a restaurant. Remember, when you score, you do less and more. You eat less, but more nutritional foods. This is what we call *Nutri-Power*. It is the cornucopia of vim and vigor that comes from healthy foods digested in moderation. Ideally, the average person should drink about half of their body weight in ounces of water each day. This type of habit allows your body to adequately cleanse itself. Failing to consume the proper amount of water means you are clogging your body, not cleansing it. Clogging is uncomfortable and debilitating. In addition, not drinking a sufficient quantity of water each day can leave you dehydrated, causing sloth and weakness. For you see, *Hydro-Power* is your source of daily strength and stamina that is derived from H_2O. Thus, drink, drink, and drink some more for less fatigue. Record your daily water intake on the scorecard. With all the medical advances we have made in modern society, experts tell us that we are no longer getting the proper level of nutrients in our daily diets. For this reason, the Score-More Regimen includes Nutraceuticals. They are an important dietary supplement to a healthy life. They can be critical for your body's cells to clearly talk to each other. When cells communicate with efficiency, you increase your chances for having robust health. And, the Score-More Regimen is about being healthy. We are partial to glyconutrients. This is the science of glycobiolgy and powerful health. Look it up on the internet and you determine what is best for you. Thus, we now have *Nutra-Power*. This is the personal energy that comes from dietary supplements for a power-driven life.

Exercise ~ *10 points*

Looking good, feeling good, being good, and performing powerfully will help build confidence and esteem for oneself. This right state of physical and mental conditioning is realized through the trifecta of fitness. This trio-of-health is composed of self-discipline, proper diet, and adequate exercise. Physical exercise, bah humbug! Everyone needs it, but no one likes it. We term it *Moto-Power,* the dynamic personal might manifested through running, walking, workout, jogging, aerobics, or other forms of exertion and physical activity. Each person needs bodily exertion for the sake of good health. Individually, we should select an exercise program that meets our personal needs. It would be wise and prudent to check with your doctor, speak with a professional physical therapist, and/or seek out a certified fitness trainer. In our Score-More Regimen, we use a system called jogawalkie. That is, we walk down hills and declines and jog up hills and inclines due to athletic infirmities. For the record, you should be prepared to exercise three to five times each week. Please be certain it is the right program for you for the appropriately allotted amount of time. In our Score-More Regimen, we endeavor to jogawalkie four times each week for a distance of three miles at a pace under forty-five minutes. Now, let's talk about *Wind-Power*. Air, like water, is a crucial necessity of life. And *Wind-Power* is the powerful force that appropriate breathing has on your overall well-being. Medical science tells us that there is a direct correlation between a person's health and the level of oxygen in their bloodstream. So, how can you learn to breathe more efficiently and effectively? Proper breathing distributes vital oxygen to all the parts of your body. But, it is not only normal breathing, but also power breathing. For power breathing, one should inhale, hold, and exhale using a ratio of 1:4:2. Do this exercise three times a day, morning, noon, and night. During each session, take-hold-emit ten power breaths. To that end, power breathing will help increase your personal energy level. It assists you in becoming a power-driven person. At this juncture, let's speak to *Nuke-Power*. This is the anatomical vitality in your physique. The brain is the power generator for the body. Our physical structure has about seventy-five kilometers of power lines called nerves. Your brain sends energy over this power grid. Like your house, if the body has the power, generally everything works. If not, you know the frustration of a power failure in the neighborhood. Frankly, it is just amazing that ninety percent of our brain's energy is used for posture. What then, are the most effective ways to help increase your energy level? Eureka, you improve your posture through proper practice, fitting exercise, and by adjusting subluxations. Simply stated, subluxations are misalignments in the spine that result in nerve pressure. Some medical experts postulate that subluxations reduce nerve flow by sixty percent. These blockages drain the brain's ability to properly communicate with the body causing irksome power failures. Please visit a professional chiropractic doctor to learn about good body positions and carriages, posture exercises, and subluxations.

Reading ~ *5 points*

It is my sincerest belief that we all must grow until we die. Otherwise, our life is half empty. Thus, we constantly and continuously read, study, and learn. In the Score-More Regimen, we allocate one-and-a-half to two hours each day to reading. This period of time is distributed between cultivating our spirituality, honing our business acumen, and reading just for fun. We engage in this activity to energize our *Cellular-Power* (that which speaks to the brain), invigorate our *Psycho-Power* (this relates to our mental fitness), reinforce our *Hypo-Power* (that vague superhuman potency of mind over matter), and confirm our *Soulur-Power* (the true essence and substance of our being).

Management by Objectives ~ *3 points*

We plan our work and work our plan. And, we manage by objectives (M.B.O.). In the same day, evening, or the following morning, you score the day before. Add it up. Think through your accomplishments of the day and, if necessary, make the appropriate adjustments. From scoring, we move on to our goals and strategies for the new day. What is the plan for the new dawn? This process is described as *Mine-Power*, as in the goal mine of forethought. Finally, we determine how we have been a good steward of our *Fund-Power*. Of course, this has to do with our material possessions, money, and assets.

Relationships ~ *1 point*

Hold dear to your family, friends, and fellow-workers. Healthy homo sapiens need connections and community. Stay connected. Each and every day, make a little time to nurture your kinships. You will be a better person because of it. We label this activity *People-Power*.

Personal Time ~ *1 point*

We refer to this exercise as *Play-Power*. In the hurly-burly of life, we all need some time off to recharge our energy levels. We must rest to refocus on reality and not take life too seriously. Therefore, commit to something regularly to amuse you, take part in a game or sport, and/or engage in some sort of recreation. Some personal time-out is good for the mind, body, and spirit.

Premiums and Penalties

The Score-More Regimen has an incentive plan for diet (less food) and exercise (more calisthenics). For nutrition, you have target and actual (c) calories. Divide the target "c" by the actual, and then multiply the quotient by the budget points. The results will be an increase or decrease in the actual points earned. Here is an illustration.

Budget points	=	7	Calories	=	c
Target 'c'	=	2000	Actual 'c'	=	1500

The answer is nine (9). You have earned two (2) premium points. Reverse the target and actual 'c' and you earn two (2) penalty points. Go ahead; figure it out for yourself. It will be good practice. Now, let's look at physical exercise. Most likely, any outcomes will vary depending on how/what you establish as your exercise program. We will demonstrate the concept using jogawalkie. In jogawalkie, we have a targeted (forty-five minutes) time factor and a targeted (three miles) distance consideration.

Budget points	=	7	Time	=	t
Distance	=	d	Target 't'	=	45
Target 'd'	=	3	Actual 't'	=	40
Actual 'd'	=	3.25			

To determine our answer, we divide target 't' by actual 't,' and then we divide target 'd' by actual 'd' to arrive at two quotients. We multiply the quotients and apply that factor against the budget points. The answer is nine. Therefore, you have earned two premium points. Interchange the formula with different variables, and you will calculate a different premium or penalty number. Again, figure it out. Good luck, and we'll see you on the beach.

Power Performance

Daily Success Scorecard

Week: **8** Day: **4** Date: **2/22/2006**

Be Your Own Best Boss

Business Matters—*Nothing happens without engagement.*

Primary ~ {40 Points} **40**

1. Money Makers	Maple Leaf/CHEE	2.5
2. SAM Actions	REBA/REMBO	2.0

Secondary ~ {20 Points} **20**

1. R & D	bepossettive.com	1.0
2. Networking	TBN Luncheon	1.5

Bizyness ~ {10 Points} **10**

1. PATTs	Just4Dads	1.0
2. G & A	Banking	0.5

Nutrition—*Controlling our own destiny.*

Calories ~ {7 Points} **8**

Nutraceuticals ~ {1 Point} **1**

Hydration ~ {2 Points} **2**

Exercise—*Do it! Do it right! Do it right now!*

Physical ~ {7 Points}	Jogawalkie (3.25 @ 40)	**9**

Breathing ~ {3 Points} **3**

Reading—*The man who reads is the man who leads.* {5 Points} **5**

1. Spirituality ~ {2 Points}	Tao Te Ching
2. Business ~ {2 Points}	Listening
3. Recreation ~ {1 Point}	White

M.B.O.—*My future depends on many things, but mostly on me.* {3 Points} **3**

1. Score ~ {1 Point}	Score
2. Plan ~ {1 Point}	Plan
3. Save ~ {1 Point}	Save

Relationships—*"SMILE"* {1 Point} **1**

Personal Time—*"R & R 4me"* {1 Point} **1**

Selling = 4 to 5 hours a day

Total Daily Points ...	*"If not me, who?"*	....	103
Target for the Day ...	*"If not now, when?*	....	100

My Can-Do Chant
"I can ... I will ... I'm good!"

Food Item	Cals	Fats	Choles	Carbs	Pros
Targets	*2000*	*80*	*300*	*250*	*90*
Coffee III	60	6	24	3	3
Cheerios	110	1	1	25	2
Milk	40	1	5	5	4
Banana	105	1	1	28	2
Bread	90	1	1	18	6
Wheat Thins	100	3	1	16	2
Tomatoes	18	1	1	4	1
Dressing	20	2	5	2	1
Bacon	80	7	15	1	5
Chips	75	1	1	17	2
Beef 3 oz.	225	15	90	2	27
Corn	83	1	1	19	3
Broccoli	92	1	1	16	10
Fats & Oils	100	14	1	1	1
Oreos	100	2	1	20	1
Wine – white	140	1	1	4	1
Popcorn	240	6	1	56	8
Pops	135	1	1	33	1
TOTALS	1,813	65	152	269	80

If you <u>score</u>, you do <u>less</u> & <u>more</u>!

Quote of the Day

Be not afraid of growing slowly, be afraid of standing still.
Chinese proverb

Water

0	8✓	16✓	24✓	32✓	40✓	48✓	56✓	64✓	72✓	80✓	88✓	96	104	112	120	128

Breathing

AM	✓	Noon	✓	PM	✓

Goals

WEIGHT:	175
EXERCISE:	3 miles/45 minutes
SCORE:	2,340

"If it's to be, it's up to me!"

Power Performance
Daily Success Scorecard

Week: _____1_____   Day: _____1_____   Date: _____

Be Your Own Best Boss

Business Matters—*Nothing happens without engagement.*

    Primary ~ {40 Points} .... _____

    1. Money Makers   _____

    2. SAM Actions   _____

    Secondary ~ {20 Points}   .... _____

    1. R & D   _____

    2. Networking   _____

    Bizyness ~ {10 Points}   .... _____

    1. PATTs   _____

    2. G & A   _____

Nutrition—*Controlling our own destiny.*

    Calories ~ {7 Points}... _____

    Nutraceuticals ~ {1 Point}.. _____

    Hydration ~ {2 Points} .... _____

Exercise—*Do it! Do it right! Do it right now!*

    Physical ~ {7 Points}   _____ _____

    Breathing ~ {3 Points} .... _____

Reading—*The man who reads is the man who leads.*   {5 Points} .... _____

    1. Spirituality ~ {2 Points}   _____

    2. Business ~ {2 Points}   _____

    3. Recreation ~ {1 Point}   _____

M.B.O.—*My future depends on many things, but mostly on me.*   {3 Points} ....

    1. Score ~ {1 Point}   _____

    2. Plan ~ {1 Point}   _____

    3. Save ~ {1 Point}   _____

Relationships—*"SMILE"*   {1 Point} .... _____

Personal Time—*"R & R 4me"*   {1 Point} .... _____

Selling = 4 to 5 hours a day

Total Daily Points ...   *"If not me, who?"*   .... _____

Target for the Day ...   *"If not now, when?*   .... _____

MY CAN-DO CHANT
"I can … I will … I'm good!"

FOOD ITEM	CALS	FATS	CHOLES	CARBS	PROS
Targets	*2000*	*80*	*300*	*250*	*90*
TOTALS					

If you <u>score</u>, you do <u>less</u> & <u>more</u>!

QUOTE OF THE DAY

"My life changed the day I realized there was a need for change in my life."
Richard Possett

WATER

8	24	40	56	72	88	104	120
0	16	32	48	64	80	96	112	128

BREATHING

AM		Noon		PM	

GOALS

WEIGHT:	_____
EXERCISE:	_____
SCORE:	_____

"If it's to be, it's up to me!"

Power Performance
Daily Success Scorecard

Week: _____1_____ Day: _____2_____ Date: _____

Be Your Own Best Boss

Business Matters—*Nothing happens without engagement.*

    Primary ~ {40 Points} .... _____

    1. Money Makers _____

    2. SAM Actions _____

    Secondary ~ {20 Points}   .... _____

    1. R & D _____

    2. Networking _____

    Bizyness ~ {10 Points}   .... _____

    1. PATTs _____

    2. G & A _____

Nutrition—*Controlling our own destiny.*

    Calories ~ {7 Points}.. _____

    Nutraceuticals ~ {1 Point}... _____

    Hydration ~ {2 Points} .... _____

Exercise—*Do it! Do it right! Do it right now!*

    Physical ~ {7 Points} _____

    Breathing ~ {3 Points} .... _____

Reading—*The man who reads is the man who leads.*   {5 Points} .... _____

    1. Spirituality ~ {2 Points} _____

    2. Business ~ {2 Points} _____

    3. Recreation ~ {1 Point} _____

M.B.O.—*My future depends on many things, but mostly on me.*   {3 Points} .... _____

    1. Score ~ {1 Point} _____

    2. Plan ~ {1 Point} _____

    3. Save ~ {1 Point} _____

Relationships—*"SMILE"*   {1 Point}......... _____

Personal Time—*"R & R 4me"*   {1 Point}......... _____

Selling = 4 to 5 hours a day

Total Daily Points ...   *"If not me, who?"*   .... _____

Target for the Day ...   *"If not now, when?*   .... _____

MY CAN-DO CHANT
"I can ... I will ... I'm good!"

FOOD ITEM	CALS	FATS	CHOLES	CARBS	PROS
Targets	*2000*	*80*	*300*	*250*	*90*
TOTALS					

If you <u>score</u>, you do <u>less</u> & <u>more</u>!

QUOTE OF THE DAY

"One does not discover new lands without consenting to lose sight of the shore for a very long time."
Andre Gide

WATER

8	24	40	56	72	88	104	120
0	16	32	48	64	80	96	112	128

BREATHING

AM		Noon		PM	

GOALS

WEIGHT: _____
EXERCISE: _____
SCORE: _____

"If it's to be, it's up to me!"

Power Performance

Daily Success Scorecard

Week: _____1_____   Day: _____3_____   Date: _____

Be Your Own Best Boss

<u>**Business Matters**</u>—*Nothing happens without engagement.*

Primary ~ {40 Points} .... _____

1. Money Makers _____

2. SAM Actions _____

Secondary ~ {20 Points}   .... _____

1. R & D _____

2. Networking _____

Bizyness ~ {10 Points}   .... _____

1. PATTs _____

2. G & A _____

<u>**Nutrition**</u>—*Controlling our own destiny.*

Calories ~ {7 Points}.. _____

Nutraceuticals ~ {1 Point}.. _____

Hydration ~ {2 Points} .... _____

<u>**Exercise**</u>—*Do it! Do it right! Do it right now!*

Physical ~ {7 Points} _____ _____

Breathing ~ {3 Points} .... _____

<u>**Reading**</u>—*The man who reads is the man who leads.*   {5 Points} .... _____

1. Spirituality ~ {2 Points} _____

2. Business ~ {2 Points} _____

3. Recreation ~ {1 Point} _____

<u>**M.B.O.**</u>—*My future depends on many things, but mostly on me.*   {3 Points} .... _____

1. Score ~ {1 Point} _____

2. Plan ~ {1 Point} _____

3. Save ~ {1 Point} _____

<u>**Relationships**</u>—*"SMILE"*   {1 Point} .... _____

<u>**Personal Time**</u>—*"R & R 4me"*   {1 Point} .... _____

Selling = 4 to 5 hours a day

Total Daily Points ...   *"If not me, who?"*   .... _____

Target for the Day ...   *"If not now, when?*   .... _____

MY CAN-DO CHANT
"I can … I will … I'm good!"

FOOD ITEM	CALS	FATS	CHOLES	CARBS	PROS
Targets	*2000*	*80*	*300*	*250*	*90*
TOTALS					

If you <u>score</u>, you do <u>less</u> & <u>more</u>!

QUOTE OF THE DAY

"A year from now you will wish you had started today."
Karen Lamb

WATER

8	24	40	56	72	88	104	120
0	16	32	48	64	80	96	112	128

BREATHING

AM		Noon		PM	

GOALS

WEIGHT: _____
EXERCISE: _____
SCORE: _____

"If it's to be, it's up to me!"

6

Power Performance

Daily Success Scorecard

Week: _____1_____   Day: _____4_____   Date: _____

Be Your Own Best Boss

Business Matters—*Nothing happens without engagement.*

Primary ~ {40 Points} .... _____

  1. Money Makers   _____

  2. SAM Actions   _____

Secondary ~ {20 Points}   .... _____

  1. R & D   _____

  2. Networking   _____

Bizyness ~ {10 Points}   .... _____

  1. PATTs   _____

  2. G & A   _____

Nutrition—*Controlling our own destiny.*

Calories ~ {7 Points}.. _____

Nutraceuticals ~ {1 Point}... _____

Hydration ~ {2 Points} .... _____

Exercise—*Do it! Do it right! Do it right now!*

Physical ~ {7 Points}   _____ _____

Breathing ~ {3 Points} .... _____

Reading—*The man who reads is the man who leads.*   {5 Points} .... _____

  1. Spirituality ~ {2 Points}   _____

  2. Business ~ {2 Points}   _____

  3. Recreation ~ {1 Point}   _____

M.B.O.—*My future depends on many things, but mostly on me.*   {3 Points} .... _____

  1. Score ~ {1 Point}   _____

  2. Plan ~ {1 Point}   _____

  3. Save ~ {1 Point}   _____

Relationships—*"SMILE"*   {1 Point}......... _____

Personal Time—*"R & R 4me"*   {1 Point}......... _____

Selling = 4 to 5 hours a day

Total Daily Points ... *"If not me, who?"*   .... _____

Target for the Day ... *"If not now, when?*   .... _____

My Can-Do Chant
"I can ... I will ... I'm good!"

Food Item	Cals	Fats	Choles	Carbs	Pros
Targets	*2000*	*80*	*300*	*250*	*90*
Totals					

If you <u>score</u>, you do <u>less</u> & more!

Quote of the Day

"You don't have to see the top of the staircase to take the first step."
Martin Luther King

Water

8	24	40	56	72	88	104	120
0	16	32	48	64	80	96	112	128

Breathing

AM		Noon		PM	

Goals

Weight: _____
Exercise: _____
Score: _____

"If it's to be, it's up to me!"

Personal
Power Performance
Daily Success Scorecard

Week: ___1___   Day: ___5___   Date: _____

Be Your Own Best Boss

<u>Business Matters</u>—*Nothing happens without engagement.*

Primary ~ {40 Points} .... _____
1. Money Makers   _____
2. SAM Actions   _____
Secondary ~ {20 Points}   .... _____
1. R & D   _____
2. Networking   _____
Bizyness ~ {10 Points}   .... _____
1. PATTs   _____
2. G & A   _____

<u>Nutrition</u>—*Controlling our own destiny.*

Calories ~ {7 Points} .... _____
Nutraceuticals ~ {1 Point} .... _____
Hydration ~ {2 Points} .... _____

<u>Exercise</u>—*Do it! Do it right! Do it right now!*

Physical ~ {7 Points}   _____ _____
Breathing ~ {3 Points} .... _____

<u>Reading</u>—*The man who reads is the man who leads.*   {5 Points} .... _____
1. Spirituality ~ {2 Points}   _____
2. Business ~ {2 Points}   _____
3. Recreation ~ {1 Point}   _____

<u>M.B.O.</u>—*My future depends on many things, but mostly on me.*   {3 Points} .... _____
1. Score ~ {1 Point}   _____
2. Plan ~ {1 Point}   _____
3. Save ~ {1 Point}   _____

<u>Relationships</u>—*"SMILE"*   {1 Point} .... _____
<u>Personal Time</u>—*"R & R 4me"*   {1 Point} .... _____

Selling = 4 to 5 hours a day

Total Daily Points ...   *"If not me, who?"*   .... **_____**
Target for the Day ...   *"If not now, when?*   .... **_____**

MY CAN-DO CHANT
"I can ... I will ... I'm good!"

FOOD ITEM	CALS	FATS	CHOLES	CARBS	PROS
Targets	2000	80	300	250	90
TOTALS					

If you <u>score</u>, you do <u>less</u> & <u>more</u>!

QUOTE OF THE DAY

"The first and best victory is to conquer self."
Plato

WATER

8	24	40	56	72	88	104	120
0	16	32	48	64	80	96	112	128

BREATHING

AM		Noon		PM	

GOALS

WEIGHT: _____
EXERCISE: _____
SCORE: _____

"If it's to be, it's up to me!"

10

Personal
Power Performance
Daily Success Scorecard

Week: ___1___   Day: ___6___   Date: _____

Be Your Own Best Boss

Business Matters—*Nothing happens without engagement.*

    Primary ~ {40 Points} .... _____

    1. Money Makers   _____

    2. SAM Actions   _____

    Secondary ~ {20 Points}   .... _____

    1. R & D   _____

    2. Networking   _____

    Bizyness ~ {10 Points}   .... _____

    1. PATTs   _____

    2. G & A   _____

Nutrition—*Controlling our own destiny.*

    Calories ~ {7 Points}.. _____

    Nutraceuticals ~ {1 Point}................................. _____

    Hydration ~ {2 Points} .... _____

Exercise—*Do it! Do it right! Do it right now!*

    Physical ~ {7 Points}   _____ _____

    Breathing ~ {3 Points} .... _____

Reading—*The man who reads is the man who leads.*   {5 Points} .... _____

    1. Spirituality ~ {2 Points}   _____

    2. Business ~ {2 Points}   _____

    3. Recreation ~ {1 Point}   _____

M.B.O.—*My future depends on many things, but mostly on me.*   {3 Points} .... _____

    1. Score ~ {1 Point}   _____

    2. Plan ~ {1 Point}   _____

    3. Save ~ {1 Point}   _____

Relationships—*"SMILE"*   {1 Point} .... _____

Personal Time—*"R & R 4me"*   {1 Point} .... _____

Selling = 4 to 5 hours a day

Total Daily Points ...   *"If not me, who?"*   .... _____

Target for the Day ...   *"If not now, when?*   .... _____

11

My Can-Do Chant
"I can … I will … I'm good!"

FOOD ITEM	CALS	FATS	CHOLES	CARBS	PROS
Targets	*2000*	*80*	*300*	*250*	*90*
TOTALS					

If you <u>score</u>, you do <u>less</u> & <u>more</u>!

QUOTE OF THE DAY

"Progress begins with the belief that what is necessary is possible."
Norman Cousins

WATER

0	8	16	24	32	40	48	56	64	72	80	88	96	104	112	120	128

BREATHING

AM		Noon		PM	

GOALS

WEIGHT: _____
EXERCISE: _____
SCORE: _____

"If it's to be, it's up to me!"

Personal

Power Performance

Daily Success Scorecard

Week: ___1___   Day: ___7___   Date: _____

Be Your Own Best Boss

Business Matters—*Nothing happens without engagement.*

   Primary ~ {40 Points} .... _____
   1. Money Makers   _____
   2. SAM Actions   _____
   Secondary ~ {20 Points}   .... _____
   1. R & D   _____
   2. Networking   _____
   Bizyness ~ {10 Points}   .... _____
   1. PATTs   _____
   2. G & A   _____

Nutrition—*Controlling our own destiny.*

   Calories ~ {7 Points} .... _____
   Nutraceuticals ~ {1 Point} .... _____
   Hydration ~ {2 Points} .... _____

Exercise—*Do it! Do it right! Do it right now!*

   Physical ~ {7 Points}   _____
   Breathing ~ {3 Points} .... _____

Reading—*The man who reads is the man who leads.*   {5 Points} .... _____

   1. Spirituality ~ {2 Points}   _____
   2. Business ~ {2 Points}   _____
   3. Recreation ~ {1 Point}   _____

M.B.O.—*My future depends on many things, but mostly on me.*   {3 Points} .... _____

   1. Score ~ {1 Point}   _____
   2. Plan ~ {1 Point}   _____
   3. Save ~ {1 Point}   _____

Relationships—*"SMILE"*   {1 Point} .... _____

Personal Time—*"R & R 4me"*   {1 Point} .... _____

Selling = 4 to 5 hours a day

Total Daily Points ...   *"If not me, who?"*   .... _____

Target for the Day ...   *"If not now, when?*   .... _____

My Can-Do Chant
"I can ... I will ... I'm good!"

Food Item	Cals	Fats	Choles	Carbs	Pros
Targets	*2000*	*80*	*300*	*250*	*90*
Totals					

If you <u>score</u>, you do <u>less</u> & <u>more!</u>

Quote of the Day

"I believe one of the most important priorities is to do whatever we do as well as we can."
Victor Kermit Kiam

Water

8	24	40	56	72	88	104	120
0	16	32	48	64	80	96	112	128

Breathing

AM		Noon		PM	

Goals

Weight:	_____
Exercise:	_____
Score:	_____

"If it's to be, it's up to me!"

Power Performance

Daily Success Scorecard

Week: _____ 2 _____   Day: _____ 1 _____   Date: _____

Be Your Own Best Boss

Business Matters—*Nothing happens without engagement.*

     Primary ~ {40 Points} .... _____
     1. Money Makers   _____
     2. SAM Actions   _____
     Secondary ~ {20 Points}   .... _____
     1. R & D   _____
     2. Networking   _____
     Bizyness ~ {10 Points}   .... _____
     1. PATTs   _____
     2. G & A   _____

Nutrition—*Controlling our own destiny.*

     Calories ~ {7 Points} .... _____
     Nutraceuticals ~ {1 Point} .... _____
     Hydration ~ {2 Points} .... _____

Exercise—*Do it! Do it right! Do it right now!*

     Physical ~ {7 Points}   _____ _____
     Breathing ~ {3 Points} .... _____

Reading—*The man who reads is the man who leads.*   {5 Points} .... _____

     1. Spirituality ~ {2 Points}   _____
     2. Business ~ {2 Points}   _____
     3. Recreation ~ {1 Point}   _____

M.B.O.—*My future depends on many things, but mostly on me.*   {3 Points} .... _____

     1. Score ~ {1 Point}   _____
     2. Plan ~ {1 Point}   _____
     3. Save ~ {1 Point}   _____

Relationships—*"SMILE"*   {1 Point} .... _____
Personal Time—*"R & R 4me"*   {1 Point} .... _____

Selling = 4 to 5 hours a day

Total Daily Points ...   *"If not me, who?"*   .... _____
Target for the Day ...   *"If not now, when?"*   .... _____

My Can-Do Chant
"I can ... I will ... I'm good!"

Food Item	Cals	Fats	Choles	Carbs	Pros
Targets	*2000*	*80*	*300*	*250*	*90*
Totals					

If you <u>score</u>, you do <u>less</u> & <u>more</u>!

Quote of the Day

"Obstacles are those frightful things you see when you take your eyes off your goal."
Henry Ford

Water

8	24	40	56	72	88	104	120
0	16	32	48	64	80	96	112	128

Breathing

AM		Noon		PM	

Goals

Weight:	
Exercise:	
Score:	

"If it's to be, it's up to me!"

Power Performance
Daily Success Scorecard

Week: ___2___   Day: ___2___   Date: _____

Be Your Own Best Boss

Business Matters—*Nothing happens without engagement.*

Primary ~ {40 Points} .... _____
1. Money Makers   _____
2. SAM Actions   _____

Secondary ~ {20 Points}   .... _____
1. R & D   _____
2. Networking   _____

Bizyness ~ {10 Points}   .... _____
1. PATTs   _____
2. G & A   _____

Nutrition—*Controlling our own destiny.*

Calories ~ {7 Points}... _____
Nutraceuticals ~ {1 Point}.. _____
Hydration ~ {2 Points} .... _____

Exercise—*Do it! Do it right! Do it right now!*

Physical ~ {7 Points}   _____ _____
Breathing ~ {3 Points} .... _____

Reading—*The man who reads is the man who leads.*   {5 Points} .... _____
1. Spirituality ~ {2 Points}   _____
2. Business ~ {2 Points}   _____
3. Recreation ~ {1 Point}   _____

M.B.O.—*My future depends on many things, but mostly on me.*   {3 Points} .... _____
1. Score ~ {1 Point}   _____
2. Plan ~ {1 Point}   _____
3. Save ~ {1 Point}   _____

Relationships—*"SMILE"*   {1 Point}......... _____
Personal Time—*"R & R 4me"*   {1 Point}......... _____

Selling = 4 to 5 hours a day

Total Daily Points ...   *"If not me, who?"*   .... _____
Target for the Day ...   *"If not now, when?"*   .... _____

My Can-Do Chant
"I can … I will … I'm good!"

FOOD ITEM	CALS	FATS	CHOLES	CARBS	PROS
Targets	*2000*	*80*	*300*	*250*	*90*
TOTALS					

If you <u>score</u>, you do <u>less</u> & <u>more</u>!

QUOTE OF THE DAY

"I do the best I know how, the very best I can, and I mean to keep doing so until the end."
Abraham Lincoln

WATER

8	24	40	56	72	88	104	120
0	16	32	48	64	80	96	112	128

BREATHING

AM		Noon		PM	

GOALS

WEIGHT: _____
EXERCISE: _____
SCORE: _____

"If it's to be, it's up to me!"

18

Personal
Power Performance
Daily Success Scorecard

Week: ____2____   Day: ____3____   Date: _____

Be Your Own Best Boss

Business Matters—*Nothing happens without engagement.*

Primary ~ {40 Points} .... _____
1. Money Makers _____
2. SAM Actions _____
Secondary ~ {20 Points} .... _____
1. R & D _____
2. Networking _____
Bizyness ~ {10 Points} .... _____
1. PATTs _____
2. G & A _____

Nutrition—*Controlling our own destiny.*

Calories ~ {7 Points}.. _____
Nutraceuticals ~ {1 Point}.. _____
Hydration ~ {2 Points} .... _____

Exercise—*Do it! Do it right! Do it right now!*

Physical ~ {7 Points} _____
Breathing ~ {3 Points} .... _____

Reading—*The man who reads is the man who leads.*   {5 Points} .... _____
1. Spirituality ~ {2 Points} _____
2. Business ~ {2 Points} _____
3. Recreation ~ {1 Point} _____

M.B.O.—*My future depends on many things, but mostly on me.*   {3 Points} .... _____
1. Score ~ {1 Point} _____
2. Plan ~ {1 Point} _____
3. Save ~ {1 Point} _____

Relationships—*"SMILE"*   {1 Point} .... _____
Personal Time—*"R & R 4me"*   {1 Point} .... _____

Selling = 4 to 5 hours a day

Total Daily Points ...   *"If not me, who?"*   .... _____
Target for the Day ...   *"If not now, when?*   .... _____

MY CAN-DO CHANT
"I can ... I will ... I'm good!"

FOOD ITEM	CALS	FATS	CHOLES	CARBS	PROS
Targets	*2000*	*80*	*300*	*250*	*90*
TOTALS					

If you <u>score</u>, you do <u>less</u> & <u>more</u>!

QUOTE OF THE DAY

"Persistent people begin their success where others end in failure."
Edward Eggleston

WATER

8	24	40	56	72	88	104	120
0	16	32	48	64	80	96	112	128

BREATHING

AM		Noon		PM	

GOALS

WEIGHT: _____
EXERCISE: _____
SCORE: _____

"If it's to be, it's up to me!"

Power Performance
Daily Success Scorecard

Week: ___2___   Day: ___4___   Date: _____

Be Your Own Best Boss

Business Matters—*Nothing happens without engagement.*

    Primary ~ {40 Points} .... _____

    1. Money Makers   _____

    2. SAM Actions   _____

    Secondary ~ {20 Points}   .... _____

    1. R & D   _____

    2. Networking   _____

    Bizyness ~ {10 Points}   .... _____

    1. PATTs   _____

    2. G & A   _____

Nutrition—*Controlling our own destiny.*

    Calories ~ {7 Points}.. _____

    Nutraceuticals ~ {1 Point}... _____

    Hydration ~ {2 Points} .... _____

Exercise—*Do it! Do it right! Do it right now!*

    Physical ~ {7 Points}   _____ _____

    Breathing ~ {3 Points} .... _____

Reading—*The man who reads is the man who leads.*   {5 Points} ....

    1. Spirituality ~ {2 Points}   _____

    2. Business ~ {2 Points}   _____

    3. Recreation ~ {1 Point}   _____

M.B.O.—*My future depends on many things, but mostly on me.*   {3 Points} ....

    1. Score ~ {1 Point}   _____

    2. Plan ~ {1 Point}   _____

    3. Save ~ {1 Point}   _____

Relationships—*"SMILE"*   {1 Point}.........

Personal Time—*"R & R 4me"*   {1 Point}.........

Selling = 4 to 5 hours a day

Total Daily Points ...   *"If not me, who?"*   .... _____

Target for the Day ...   *"If not now, when?"*   .... _____

My Can-Do Chant
"I can ... I will ... I'm good!"

FOOD ITEM	CALS	FATS	CHOLES	CARBS	PROS
Targets	*2000*	*80*	*300*	*250*	*90*
TOTALS					

If you <u>score</u>, you do <u>less</u> & <u>more</u>!

QUOTE OF THE DAY

"It takes courage to grow up and become who you really are."
E. E. Cummings

WATER

8	24	40	56	72	88	104	120
0 16	32	48	64	80	96	112	128

BREATHING

AM		Noon		PM	

GOALS

WEIGHT: _____
EXERCISE: _____
SCORE: _____

"If it's to be, it's up to me!"

Power Performance
Daily Success Scorecard

Week: ___2___   Day: ___5___   Date: _____

Be Your Own Best Boss

Business Matters—*Nothing happens without engagement.*

  Primary ~ {40 Points} .... _____
  1. Money Makers   _____
  2. SAM Actions   _____
  Secondary ~ {20 Points}   .... _____
  1. R & D   _____
  2. Networking   _____
  Bizyness ~ {10 Points}   .... _____
  1. PATTs   _____
  2. G & A   _____

Nutrition—*Controlling our own destiny.*

  Calories ~ {7 Points} .... _____
  Nutraceuticals ~ {1 Point} .... _____
  Hydration ~ {2 Points} .... _____

Exercise—*Do it! Do it right! Do it right now!*

  Physical ~ {7 Points}   _____ _____
  Breathing ~ {3 Points} .... _____

Reading—*The man who reads is the man who leads.*   {5 Points} .... _____
  1. Spirituality ~ {2 Points}   _____
  2. Business ~ {2 Points}   _____
  3. Recreation ~ {1 Point}   _____

M.B.O.—*My future depends on many things, but mostly on me.*   {3 Points} .... _____
  1. Score ~ {1 Point}   _____
  2. Plan ~ {1 Point}   _____
  3. Save ~ {1 Point}   _____

Relationships—*"SMILE"*   {1 Point} .... _____

Personal Time—*"R & R 4me"*   {1 Point} .... _____

Selling = 4 to 5 hours a day

Total Daily Points ...   *"If not me, who?"*   .... _____

Target for the Day ...   *"If not now, when?*   .... _____

My Can-Do Chant
"I can ... I will ... I'm good!"

Food Item	Cals	Fats	Choles	Carbs	Pros
Targets	*2000*	*80*	*300*	*250*	*90*
Totals					

If you <u>score</u>, you do <u>less</u> & <u>more</u>!

Quote of the Day
"Talent without discipline is like an octopus on roller skates. There's plenty of movement, but you never know if it's going to be forward, backwards, or sideways."

H. Jackson Brown, Jr.

Water

8	24	40	56	72	88	104	120
0 16	32	48	64	80	96	112	128

Breathing

AM		Noon		PM	

Goals

WEIGHT: _____
EXERCISE: _____
SCORE: _____

"If it's to be, it's up to me!"

Personal
Power Performance
Daily Success Scorecard

Week: _____ 2 _____   Day: _____ 6 _____   Date: _____

Be Your Own Best Boss

Business Matters—*Nothing happens without engagement.*

Primary ~ {40 Points} .... _____

1. Money Makers _____

2. SAM Actions _____

Secondary ~ {20 Points} .... _____

1. R & D _____

2. Networking _____

Bizyness ~ {10 Points} .... _____

1. PATTs _____

2. G & A _____

Nutrition—*Controlling our own destiny.*

Calories ~ {7 Points}.. _____

Nutraceuticals ~ {1 Point}.. _____

Hydration ~ {2 Points} .... _____

Exercise—*Do it! Do it right! Do it right now!*

Physical ~ {7 Points} _____ _____

Breathing ~ {3 Points} .... _____

Reading—*The man who reads is the man who leads.*   {5 Points} .... _____

1. Spirituality ~ {2 Points} _____

2. Business ~ {2 Points} _____

3. Recreation ~ {1 Point} _____

M.B.O.—*My future depends on many things, but mostly on me.*   {3 Points} .... _____

1. Score ~ {1 Point} _____

2. Plan ~ {1 Point} _____

3. Save ~ {1 Point} _____

Relationships—*"SMILE"*   {1 Point} .... _____

Personal Time—*"R & R 4me"*   {1 Point} .... _____

Selling = 4 to 5 hours a day

Total Daily Points ...   *"If not me, who?"*   .... _____

Target for the Day ...   *"If not now, when?*   .... _____

MY CAN-DO CHANT
"I can ... I will ... I'm good!"

FOOD ITEM	CALS	FATS	CHOLES	CARBS	PROS
Targets	*2000*	*80*	*300*	*250*	*90*
TOTALS					

If you <u>score</u>, you do <u>less</u> & <u>more</u>!

QUOTE OF THE DAY

"A good try only counts in the game of rugby."
Vanposetski

WATER

8	24	40	56	72	88	104	120
0	16	32	48	64	80	96	112	128

BREATHING

AM		Noon		PM	

GOALS

WEIGHT:	_____
EXERCISE:	_____
SCORE:	_____

"If it's to be, it's up to me!"

Power Performance

Daily Success Scorecard

Week: ___2___   Day: ___7___   Date: _____

Be Your Own Best Boss

Business Matters—*Nothing happens without engagement.*

    Primary ~ {40 Points} .... _____

    1. Money Makers   _____

    2. SAM Actions   _____

    Secondary ~ {20 Points}   .... _____

    1. R & D   _____

    2. Networking   _____

    Bizyness ~ {10 Points}   .... _____

    1. PATTs   _____

    2. G & A   _____

Nutrition—*Controlling our own destiny.*

    Calories ~ {7 Points} .... _____

    Nutraceuticals ~ {1 Point} .... _____

    Hydration ~ {2 Points} .... _____

Exercise—*Do it! Do it right! Do it right now!*

    Physical ~ {7 Points}   _____ _____

    Breathing ~ {3 Points} .... _____

Reading—*The man who reads is the man who leads.*   {5 Points} .... _____

    1. Spirituality ~ {2 Points}   _____

    2. Business ~ {2 Points}   _____

    3. Recreation ~ {1 Point}   _____

M.B.O.—*My future depends on many things, but mostly on me.*   {3 Points} .... _____

    1. Score ~ {1 Point}   _____

    2. Plan ~ {1 Point}   _____

    3. Save ~ {1 Point}   _____

Relationships—*"SMILE"*   {1 Point} .... _____

Personal Time—*"R & R 4me"*   {1 Point} .... _____

Selling = 4 to 5 hours a day

Total Daily Points ...   *"If not me, who?"*   .... _____

Target for the Day ...   *"If not now, when?"*   .... _____

My Can-Do Chant
"I can … I will … I'm good!"

Food Item	Cals	Fats	Choles	Carbs	Pros
Targets	*2000*	*80*	*300*	*250*	*90*
Totals					

If you <u>score</u>, you do <u>less</u> & <u>more</u>!

Quote of the Day
"Some twenty years her senior, he preserved a gift that she supposed herself to have already lost-not youth's creative power, but its self-confidence and optimism."

E. M. Forster

Water

8	24	40	56	72	88	104	120
0	16	32	48	64	80	96	112	128

Breathing

AM		Noon		PM	

Goals

Weight:	_____
Exercise:	_____
Score:	_____

"If it's to be, it's up to me!"

Power Performance
Daily Success Scorecard

Week: ___3___   Day: ___1___   Date: _____

Be Your Own Best Boss

Business Matters—*Nothing happens without engagement.*

Primary ~ {40 Points} .... _____
1. Money Makers _____
2. SAM Actions _____
Secondary ~ {20 Points} .... _____
1. R & D _____
2. Networking _____
Bizyness ~ {10 Points} .... _____
1. PATTs _____
2. G & A _____

Nutrition—*Controlling our own destiny.*

Calories ~ {7 Points}.. _____
Nutraceuticals ~ {1 Point}.. _____
Hydration ~ {2 Points} .... _____

Exercise—*Do it! Do it right! Do it right now!*

Physical ~ {7 Points} _____ _____
Breathing ~ {3 Points} .... _____

Reading—*The man who reads is the man who leads.*   {5 Points} .... _____
1. Spirituality ~ {2 Points} _____
2. Business ~ {2 Points} _____
3. Recreation ~ {1 Point} _____

M.B.O.—*My future depends on many things, but mostly on me.*   {3 Points} .... _____
1. Score ~ {1 Point} _____
2. Plan ~ {1 Point} _____
3. Save ~ {1 Point} _____

Relationships—*"SMILE"*   {1 Point} .... _____
Personal Time—*"R & R 4me"*   {1 Point} .... _____

Selling = 4 to 5 hours a day

Total Daily Points ...   *"If not me, who?"*   .... _____
Target for the Day ...   *"If not now, when?*   .... _____

MY CAN-DO CHANT
"I can … I will … I'm good!"

FOOD ITEM	CALS	FATS	CHOLES	CARBS	PROS
Targets	*2000*	*80*	*300*	*250*	*90*
TOTALS					

If you <u>score</u>, you do <u>less</u> & <u>more</u>!

QUOTE OF THE DAY

"Be responsible for yourself."
Peter Biadasz

WATER

8	24	40	56	72	88	104	120
0	16	32	48	64	80	96	112	128

BREATHING

AM		Noon		PM	

GOALS

WEIGHT: _____
EXERCISE: _____
SCORE: _____

"If it's to be, it's up to me!"

30

Power Performance
Daily Success Scorecard

Week: _____3_____   Day: _____2_____   Date: _____

Be Your Own Best Boss

Business Matters—*Nothing happens without engagement.*

Primary ~ {40 Points} .... _____

1. Money Makers   _____

2. SAM Actions   _____

Secondary ~ {20 Points}   .... _____

1. R & D   _____

2. Networking   _____

Bizyness ~ {10 Points}   .... _____

1. PATTs   _____

2. G & A   _____

Nutrition—*Controlling our own destiny.*

Calories ~ {7 Points}.. _____

Nutraceuticals ~ {1 Point}.................................... _____

Hydration ~ {2 Points} .... _____

Exercise—*Do it! Do it right! Do it right now!*

Physical ~ {7 Points}   _____

Breathing ~ {3 Points} .... _____

Reading—*The man who reads is the man who leads.*   {5 Points} .... _____

1. Spirituality ~ {2 Points}   _____

2. Business ~ {2 Points}   _____

3. Recreation ~ {1 Point}   _____

M.B.O.—*My future depends on many things, but mostly on me.*   {3 Points} .... _____

1. Score ~ {1 Point}   _____

2. Plan ~ {1 Point}   _____

3. Save ~ {1 Point}   _____

Relationships—*"SMILE"*   {1 Point}......... _____

Personal Time—*"R & R 4me"*   {1 Point}......... _____

Selling = 4 to 5 hours a day

Total Daily Points ...   *"If not me, who?"*   .... _____

Target for the Day ...   *"If not now, when?*   .... _____

MY CAN-DO CHANT
"I can ... I will ... I'm good!"

FOOD ITEM	CALS	FATS	CHOLES	CARBS	PROS
Targets	*2000*	*80*	*300*	*250*	*90*
TOTALS					

If you <u>score</u>, you do <u>less</u> & <u>more!</u>

QUOTE OF THE DAY

"There's no better time than the present to be better than we were yesterday."
Gary Kelly

WATER

8	24	40	56	72	88	104	120
0	16	32	48	64	80	96	112	128

BREATHING

AM		Noon		PM	

GOALS

WEIGHT: _____
EXERCISE: _____
SCORE: _____

"If it's to be, it's up to me!"

Personal
Power Performance
Daily Success Scorecard

Week: _____ 3 _____ Day: _____ 3 _____ Date: _____

Be Your Own Best Boss

Business Matters—*Nothing happens without engagement.*

    Primary ~ {40 Points} .... _____

    1. Money Makers   _____

    2. SAM Actions   _____

    Secondary ~ {20 Points}   .... _____

    1. R & D   _____

    2. Networking   _____

    Bizyness ~ {10 Points}   .... _____

    1. PATTs   _____

    2. G & A   _____

Nutrition—*Controlling our own destiny.*

    Calories ~ {7 Points} .... _____

    Nutraceuticals ~ {1 Point} .... _____

    Hydration ~ {2 Points} .... _____

Exercise—*Do it! Do it right! Do it right now!*

    Physical ~ {7 Points}   _____

    Breathing ~ {3 Points} .... _____

Reading—*The man who reads is the man who leads.*   {5 Points} .... _____

    1. Spirituality ~ {2 Points}   _____

    2. Business ~ {2 Points}   _____

    3. Recreation ~ {1 Point}   _____

M.B.O.—*My future depends on many things, but mostly on me.*   {3 Points} .... _____

    1. Score ~ {1 Point}   _____

    2. Plan ~ {1 Point}   _____

    3. Save ~ {1 Point}   _____

Relationships—*"SMILE"*   {1 Point} .... _____

Personal Time—*"R & R 4me"*   {1 Point} .... _____

Selling = 4 to 5 hours a day

Total Daily Points ...   *"If not me, who?"*   .... _____

Target for the Day ...   *"If not now, when?*"   .... _____

My Can-Do Chant
"I can ... I will ... I'm good!"

Food Item	Cals	Fats	Choles	Carbs	Pros
Targets	*2000*	*80*	*300*	*250*	*90*
Totals					

If you <u>score</u>, you do <u>less</u> & <u>more</u>!

Quote of the Day

"My life as a writer consists of 1/8 talent and 7/8 discipline."
John Irving

Water

8	24	40	56	72	88	104	120
0	16	32	48	64	80	96	112	128

Breathing

AM		Noon		PM	

Goals

WEIGHT: _____
EXERCISE: _____
SCORE: _____

"If it's to be, it's up to me!"

Power Performance
Daily Success Scorecard

Week: 3 Day: 4 Date: _____

Be Your Own Best Boss

Business Matters—*Nothing happens without engagement.*

Primary ~ {40 Points} .... _____
1. Money Makers _____
2. SAM Actions _____
Secondary ~ {20 Points} .... _____
1. R & D _____
2. Networking _____
Bizyness ~ {10 Points} .... _____
1. PATTs _____
2. G & A _____

Nutrition—*Controlling our own destiny.*

Calories ~ {7 Points}.. _____
Nutraceuticals ~ {1 Point}.................................... _____
Hydration ~ {2 Points} .... _____

Exercise—*Do it! Do it right! Do it right now!*

Physical ~ {7 Points} _____ _____
Breathing ~ {3 Points} .... _____

Reading—*The man who reads is the man who leads.* {5 Points} .... _____
1. Spirituality ~ {2 Points} _____
2. Business ~ {2 Points} _____
3. Recreation ~ {1 Point} _____

M.B.O.—*My future depends on many things, but mostly on me.* {3 Points} .... _____
1. Score ~ {1 Point} _____
2. Plan ~ {1 Point} _____
3. Save ~ {1 Point} _____

Relationships—*"SMILE"* {1 Point}......... _____
Personal Time—*"R & R 4me"* {1 Point}......... _____

Selling = 4 to 5 hours a day

Total Daily Points ... *"If not me, who?"* .... _____
Target for the Day ... *"If not now, when?"* .... _____

My Can-Do Chant
"I can ... I will ... I'm good!"

FOOD ITEM	CALS	FATS	CHOLES	CARBS	PROS
Targets	*2000*	*80*	*300*	*250*	*90*
TOTALS					

If you <u>score</u>, you do <u>less</u> & <u>more</u>!

QUOTE OF THE DAY

"To improve is to change; to be perfect is to change often."
Winston Churchill

WATER

8	24	40	56	72	88	104	120
0	16	32	48	64	80	96	112	128

BREATHING

AM		Noon		PM	

GOALS

WEIGHT: _____
EXERCISE: _____
SCORE: _____

"If it's to be, it's up to me!"

36

Power Performance
Daily Success Scorecard

Week: _____3_____   Day: _____5_____   Date: _____

Be Your Own Best Boss

Business Matters—*Nothing happens without engagement.*

    Primary ~ {40 Points} .... _____

    1. Money Makers   _____

    2. SAM Actions   _____

    Secondary ~ {20 Points}   .... _____

    1. R & D   _____

    2. Networking   _____

    Bizyness ~ {10 Points}   .... _____

    1. PATTs   _____

    2. G & A   _____

Nutrition—*Controlling our own destiny.*

    Calories ~ {7 Points}.. _____

    Nutraceuticals ~ {1 Point}... _____

    Hydration ~ {2 Points} .... _____

Exercise—*Do it! Do it right! Do it right now!*

    Physical ~ {7 Points}   _____

    Breathing ~ {3 Points} .... _____

Reading—*The man who reads is the man who leads.*   {5 Points} .... _____

    1. Spirituality ~ {2 Points}   _____

    2. Business ~ {2 Points}   _____

    3. Recreation ~ {1 Point}   _____

M.B.O.—*My future depends on many things, but mostly on me.*   {3 Points} .... _____

    1. Score ~ {1 Point}   _____

    2. Plan ~ {1 Point}   _____

    3. Save ~ {1 Point}   _____

Relationships—*"SMILE"*   {1 Point}......... _____

Personal Time—*"R & R 4me"*   {1 Point}......... _____

Selling = 4 to 5 hours a day

Total Daily Points ...   *"If not me, who?"*   .... _____

Target for the Day ...   *"If not now, when?*   .... _____

MY CAN-DO CHANT
"I can … I will … I'm good!"

FOOD ITEM	CALS	FATS	CHOLES	CARBS	PROS
Targets	*2000*	*80*	*300*	*250*	*90*
TOTALS					

If you <u>score</u>, you do <u>less</u> & <u>more</u>!

QUOTE OF THE DAY

"Effort only fully releases its reward after a person refuses to quit."
Napoleon Hill

WATER

8	24	40	56	72	88	104	120
0	16	32	48	64	80	96	112	128

BREATHING

AM		Noon		PM	

GOALS

WEIGHT: _____
EXERCISE: _____
SCORE: _____

"If it's to be, it's up to me!"

38

Personal
Power Performance
Daily Success Scorecard

Week: _____ 3 _____   Day: _____ 6 _____   Date: _____

Be Your Own Best Boss

Business Matters—*Nothing happens without engagement.*

    Primary ~ {40 Points} .... _____

    1. Money Makers   _____

    2. SAM Actions   _____

    Secondary ~ {20 Points}   .... _____

    1. R & D   _____

    2. Networking   _____

    Bizyness ~ {10 Points}   .... _____

    1. PATTs   _____

    2. G & A   _____

Nutrition—*Controlling our own destiny.*

    Calories ~ {7 Points}... _____

    Nutraceuticals ~ {1 Point}................................... _____

    Hydration ~ {2 Points} .... _____

Exercise—*Do it! Do it right! Do it right now!*

    Physical ~ {7 Points}   _____ _____

    Breathing ~ {3 Points} .... _____

Reading—*The man who reads is the man who leads.*   {5 Points} .... _____

    1. Spirituality ~ {2 Points}   _____

    2. Business ~ {2 Points}   _____

    3. Recreation ~ {1 Point}   _____

M.B.O.—*My future depends on many things, but mostly on me.*   {3 Points} .... _____

    1. Score ~ {1 Point}   _____

    2. Plan ~ {1 Point}   _____

    3. Save ~ {1 Point}   _____

Relationships—*"SMILE"*   {1 Point} .... _____

Personal Time—*"R & R 4me"*   {1 Point} .... _____

Selling = 4 to 5 hours a day

Total Daily Points ...   *"If not me, who?"*   .... _____

Target for the Day ...   *"If not now, when?"*   .... _____

My Can-Do Chant
"I can ... I will ... I'm good!"

Food Item	Cals	Fats	Choles	Carbs	Pros
Targets	*2000*	*80*	*300*	*250*	*90*
Totals					

If you <u>score</u>, you do <u>less</u> & <u>more</u>!

Quote of the Day

"Success is more a function of consistent common sense than it is of genius."

An Wang

Water

8	24	40	56	72	88	104	120
0	16	32	48	64	80	96	112	128

Breathing

AM		Noon		PM	

Goals

Weight:	_____
Exercise:	_____
Score:	_____

"If it's to be, it's up to me!"

Power Performance
Daily Success Scorecard

Week: ___3___   Day: ___7___   Date: _____

Be Your Own Best Boss

Business Matters—*Nothing happens without engagement.*

   Primary ~ {40 Points} .... _____
   1. Money Makers   _____
   2. SAM Actions   _____
   Secondary ~ {20 Points}   .... _____
   1. R & D   _____
   2. Networking   _____
   Bizyness ~ {10 Points}   .... _____
   1. PATTs   _____
   2. G & A   _____

Nutrition—*Controlling our own destiny.*

   Calories ~ {7 Points}.. _____
   Nutraceuticals ~ {1 Point}...................................... _____
   Hydration ~ {2 Points} .... _____

Exercise—*Do it! Do it right! Do it right now!*

   Physical ~ {7 Points}   _____ _____
   Breathing ~ {3 Points} .... _____

Reading—*The man who reads is the man who leads.*   {5 Points} .... _____
   1. Spirituality ~ {2 Points}   _____
   2. Business ~ {2 Points}   _____
   3. Recreation ~ {1 Point}   _____

M.B.O.—*My future depends on many things, but mostly on me.*   {3 Points} .... _____
   1. Score ~ {1 Point}   _____
   2. Plan ~ {1 Point}   _____
   3. Save ~ {1 Point}   _____

Relationships—*"SMILE"*   {1 Point} .... _____
Personal Time—*"R & R 4me"*   {1 Point} .... _____

Selling = 4 to 5 hours a day

Total Daily Points ...   *"If not me, who?"*   .... _____
Target for the Day ...   *"If not now, when?*   .... _____

My Can-Do Chant
"I can ... I will ... I'm good!"

FOOD ITEM	CALS	FATS	CHOLES	CARBS	PROS
Targets	*2000*	*80*	*300*	*250*	*90*
TOTALS					

If you <u>score</u>, you do <u>less</u> & <u>more</u>!

QUOTE OF THE DAY

"We must use time as a tool, not as a crutch."
John F. Kennedy

WATER

8	24	40	56	72	88	104	120
0	16	32	48	64	80	96	112	128

BREATHING

AM		Noon		PM	

GOALS

WEIGHT: _____
EXERCISE: _____
SCORE: _____

"If it's to be, it's up to me!"

Power Performance
Daily Success Scorecard

Week: ____4____   Day: ____1____   Date: _____

Be Your Own Best Boss

Business Matters—*Nothing happens without engagement.*

    Primary ~ {40 Points} .... _____

    1. Money Makers   _____

    2. SAM Actions   _____

    Secondary ~ {20 Points}   .... _____

    1. R & D   _____

    2. Networking   _____

    Bizyness ~ {10 Points}   .... _____

    1. PATTs   _____

    2. G & A   _____

Nutrition—*Controlling our own destiny.*

    Calories ~ {7 Points}.. _____

    Nutraceuticals ~ {1 Point}.................................... _____

    Hydration ~ {2 Points} .... _____

Exercise—*Do it! Do it right! Do it right now!*

    Physical ~ {7 Points}   _____ _____

    Breathing ~ {3 Points} .... _____

Reading—*The man who reads is the man who leads.*   {5 Points} .... _____

    1. Spirituality ~ {2 Points}   _____

    2. Business ~ {2 Points}   _____

    3. Recreation ~ {1 Point}   _____

_M.B.O._—*My future depends on many things, but mostly on me.*   {3 Points} .... _____

    1. Score ~ {1 Point}   _____

    2. Plan ~ {1 Point}   _____

    3. Save ~ {1 Point}   _____

Relationships—*"SMILE"*   {1 Point}......... _____

Personal Time—*"R & R 4me"*   {1 Point}......... _____

Selling = 4 to 5 hours a day

Total Daily Points ...   *"If not me, who?"*   .... _____

Target for the Day ...   *"If not now, when?"*   .... _____

MY CAN-DO CHANT
"I can ... I will ... I'm good!"

FOOD ITEM	CALS	FATS	CHOLES	CARBS	PROS
Targets	*2000*	*80*	*300*	*250*	*90*
TOTALS					

If you <u>score</u>, you do <u>less</u> & <u>more</u>!

QUOTE OF THE DAY

"Determination is often the first chapter in the book of excellence."
POZ

WATER

8	24	40	56	72	88	104	120
0	16	32	48	64	80	96	112	128

BREATHING

AM		Noon		PM	

GOALS

WEIGHT:	_____
EXERCISE:	_____
SCORE:	_____

"If it's to be, it's up to me!"

Power Performance

Daily Success Scorecard

Week: **4** Day: **2** Date: _____

Be Your Own Best Boss

Business Matters—*Nothing happens without engagement.*

Primary ~ {40 Points} .... _____

1. Money Makers _____

2. SAM Actions _____

Secondary ~ {20 Points} .... _____

1. R & D _____

2. Networking _____

Bizyness ~ {10 Points} .... _____

1. PATTs _____

2. G & A _____

Nutrition—*Controlling our own destiny.*

Calories ~ {7 Points} .... _____

Nutraceuticals ~ {1 Point} .... _____

Hydration ~ {2 Points} .... _____

Exercise—*Do it! Do it right! Do it right now!*

Physical ~ {7 Points} _____ _____

Breathing ~ {3 Points} .... _____

Reading—*The man who reads is the man who leads.* {5 Points} .... _____

1. Spirituality ~ {2 Points} _____

2. Business ~ {2 Points} _____

3. Recreation ~ {1 Point} _____

M.B.O.—*My future depends on many things, but mostly on me.* {3 Points} ....

1. Score ~ {1 Point} _____

2. Plan ~ {1 Point} _____

3. Save ~ {1 Point} _____

Relationships—*"SMILE"* {1 Point} .... _____

Personal Time—*"R & R 4me"* {1 Point} .... _____

Selling = 4 to 5 hours a day

Total Daily Points ... *"If not me, who?"* .... _____

Target for the Day ... *"If not now, when?"* .... _____

My Can-Do Chant
"I can ... I will ... I'm good!"

Food Item	Cals	Fats	Choles	Carbs	Pros
Targets	*2000*	*80*	*300*	*250*	*90*
Totals					

If you <u>score</u>, you do <u>less</u> & <u>more</u>!

Quote of the Day

"It is not enough to aim; you must hit."
Italian proverb

Water

8	24	40	56	72	88	104	120
0 16	32	48	64	80	96	112	128

Breathing

AM		Noon		PM	

Goals

Weight:	_____
Exercise:	_____
Score:	_____

"If it's to be, it's up to me!"

46

Personal
Power Performance
Daily Success Scorecard

Week: __4__   Day: __3__   Date: _____

Be Your Own Best Boss

<u>Business Matters</u>—*Nothing happens without engagement.*

    Primary ~ {40 Points} .... _____

    1. Money Makers   _____

    2. SAM Actions   _____

    Secondary ~ {20 Points}   .... _____

    1. R & D   _____

    2. Networking   _____

    Bizyness ~ {10 Points}   .... _____

    1. PATTs   _____

    2. G & A   _____

<u>Nutrition</u>—*Controlling our own destiny.*

    Calories ~ {7 Points} .... _____

    Nutraceuticals ~ {1 Point} .... _____

    Hydration ~ {2 Points} .... _____

<u>Exercise</u>—*Do it! Do it right! Do it right now!*

    Physical ~ {7 Points}   _____ _____

    Breathing ~ {3 Points} .... _____

<u>Reading</u>—*The man who reads is the man who leads.*   {5 Points} .... _____

    1. Spirituality ~ {2 Points}   _____

    2. Business ~ {2 Points}   _____

    3. Recreation ~ {1 Point}   _____

<u>M.B.O.</u>—*My future depends on many things, but mostly on me.*   {3 Points} .... _____

    1. Score ~ {1 Point}   _____

    2. Plan ~ {1 Point}   _____

    3. Save ~ {1 Point}   _____

<u>Relationships</u>—*"SMILE"*   {1 Point} .... _____

<u>Personal Time</u>—*"R & R 4me"*   {1 Point} .... _____

Selling = 4 to 5 hours a day

Total Daily Points ...   *"If not me, who?"*   .... _____

Target for the Day ...   *"If not now, when?"*   .... _____

MY CAN-DO CHANT
"I can ... I will ... I'm good!"

FOOD ITEM	CALS	FATS	CHOLES	CARBS	PROS
Targets	*2000*	*80*	*300*	*250*	*90*
TOTALS					

If you <u>score</u>, you do <u>less</u> & <u>more</u>!

QUOTE OF THE DAY

"Today we have done what we had to do. If necessary, we shall do it again."
Ronald Reagan

WATER

8	24	40	56	72	88	104	120
0 16	32	48	64	80	96	112	128

BREATHING

AM		Noon		PM	

GOALS

WEIGHT: _____
EXERCISE: _____
SCORE: _____

"If it's to be, it's up to me!"

Personal

Power Performance

Daily Success Scorecard

Week: ___4___   Day: ___4___   Date: _____

Be Your Own Best Boss

<u>**Business Matters**</u>—*Nothing happens without engagement.*

    Primary ~ {40 Points} .... _____
    1. Money Makers   _____
    2. SAM Actions   _____
    Secondary ~ {20 Points}   .... _____
    1. R & D   _____
    2. Networking   _____
    Bizyness ~ {10 Points}   .... _____
    1. PATTs   _____
    2. G & A   _____

<u>**Nutrition**</u>—*Controlling our own destiny.*

    Calories ~ {7 Points} .... _____
    Nutraceuticals ~ {1 Point} .... _____
    Hydration ~ {2 Points} .... _____

<u>**Exercise**</u>—*Do it! Do it right! Do it right now!*

    Physical ~ {7 Points}   _____ _____
    Breathing ~ {3 Points} .... _____

<u>**Reading**</u>—*The man who reads is the man who leads.*   {5 Points} .... _____

    1. Spirituality ~ {2 Points}   _____
    2. Business ~ {2 Points}   _____
    3. Recreation ~ {1 Point}   _____

<u>**M.B.O.**</u>—*My future depends on many things, but mostly on me.* {3 Points} .... _____

    1. Score ~ {1 Point}   _____
    2. Plan ~ {1 Point}   _____
    3. Save ~ {1 Point}   _____

<u>**Relationships**</u>—*"SMILE"*   {1 Point} .... _____

<u>**Personal Time**</u>—*"R & R 4me"*   {1 Point} .... _____

Selling = 4 to 5 hours a day

Total Daily Points ...   *"If not me, who?"* .... _____

Target for the Day ...   *"If not now, when?* .... _____

MY CAN-DO CHANT
"I can ... I will ... I'm good!"

FOOD ITEM	CALS	FATS	CHOLES	CARBS	PROS
Targets	*2000*	*80*	*300*	*250*	*90*
TOTALS					

If you <u>score</u>, you do <u>less</u> & <u>more!</u>

QUOTE OF THE DAY

"You become a champion by fighting one more round. When things are tough, you fight one more round."
Vanposetski

WATER

8	24	40	56	72	88	104	120
0	16	32	48	64	80	96	112	128

BREATHING

AM		Noon		PM	

GOALS

WEIGHT:	_____
EXERCISE:	_____
SCORE:	_____

"If it's to be, it's up to me!"

Personal
Power Performance
Daily Success Scorecard

Week: _____4_____ Day: _____5_____ Date: _____

Be Your Own Best Boss

Business Matters—*Nothing happens without engagement.*

    Primary ~ {40 Points} .... _____

    1. Money Makers   _____

    2. SAM Actions   _____

    Secondary ~ {20 Points}   .... _____

    1. R & D   _____

    2. Networking   _____

    Bizyness ~ {10 Points}   .... _____

    1. PATTs   _____

    2. G & A   _____

Nutrition—*Controlling our own destiny.*

    Calories ~ {7 Points}... _____

    Nutraceuticals ~ {1 Point}.................................... _____

    Hydration ~ {2 Points} .... _____

Exercise—*Do it! Do it right! Do it right now!*

    Physical ~ {7 Points}   _____ _____

    Breathing ~ {3 Points} .... _____

Reading—*The man who reads is the man who leads.*   {5 Points} .... _____

    1. Spirituality ~ {2 Points}   _____

    2. Business ~ {2 Points}   _____

    3. Recreation ~ {1 Point}

M.B.O.—*My future depends on many things, but mostly on me.*   {3 Points} .... _____

    1. Score ~ {1 Point}   _____

    2. Plan ~ {1 Point}   _____

    3. Save ~ {1 Point}   _____

Relationships—*"SMILE"*   {1 Point}......... _____

Personal Time—*"R & R 4me"*   {1 Point}......... _____

Selling = 4 to 5 hours a day

Total Daily Points ...   *"If not me, who?"*   .... _____

Target for the Day ...   *"If not now, when?"*   .... _____

My Can-Do Chant
"I can ... I will ... I'm good!"

Food Item	Cals	Fats	Choles	Carbs	Pros
Targets	*2000*	*80*	*300*	*250*	*90*
Totals					

If you <u>score</u>, you do <u>less</u> & <u>more</u>!

Quote of the Day

"Whenever we do what we can, we immediately can do more."
James Freeman Clarke

Water

8	24	40	56	72	88	104	120
0 16	32	48	64	80	96	112	128

Breathing

AM		Noon		PM	

Goals

WEIGHT:	_____
EXERCISE:	_____
SCORE:	_____

"If it's to be, it's up to me!"

Power Performance
Daily Success Scorecard

Week: _____4_____   Day: _____6_____   Date: _____

Be Your Own Best Boss

Business Matters—*Nothing happens without engagement.*

    Primary ~ {40 Points} .... _____

    1. Money Makers   _____

    2. SAM Actions   _____

    Secondary ~ {20 Points}   .... _____

    1. R & D   _____

    2. Networking   _____

    Bizyness ~ {10 Points}   .... _____

    1. PATTs   _____

    2. G & A   _____

Nutrition—*Controlling our own destiny.*

    Calories ~ {7 Points} .... _____

    Nutraceuticals ~ {1 Point} .... _____

    Hydration ~ {2 Points} .... _____

Exercise—*Do it! Do it right! Do it right now!*

    Physical ~ {7 Points}   _____

    Breathing ~ {3 Points} .... _____

Reading—*The man who reads is the man who leads.*   {5 Points} .... _____

    1. Spirituality ~ {2 Points}   _____

    2. Business ~ {2 Points}   _____

    3. Recreation ~ {1 Point}   _____

M.B.O.—*My future depends on many things, but mostly on me.*   {3 Points} .... _____

    1. Score ~ {1 Point}   _____

    2. Plan ~ {1 Point}   _____

    3. Save ~ {1 Point}   _____

Relationships—*"SMILE"*   {1 Point} .... _____

Personal Time—*"R & R 4me"*   {1 Point} .... _____

Selling = 4 to 5 hours a day

Total Daily Points ...   *"If not me, who?"*   .... **_____**

Target for the Day ...   *"If not now, when?*   .... **_____**

My Can-Do Chant
"I can … I will … I'm good!"

Food Item	Cals	Fats	Choles	Carbs	Pros
Targets	*2000*	*80*	*300*	*250*	*90*
Totals					

If you <u>score</u>, you do <u>less</u> & <u>more!</u>

Quote of the Day

"How we spend our days is, of course, how we spend our lives."
Annie Dillard

Water

8	24	40	56	72	88	104	120
0	16	32	48	64	80	96	112	128

Breathing

AM		Noon		PM	

Goals

WEIGHT: _____
EXERCISE: _____
SCORE: _____

"If it's to be, it's up to me!"

Personal
Power Performance
Daily Success Scorecard

Week: ___4___   Day: ___7___   Date: _____

Be Your Own Best Boss

Business Matters—*Nothing happens without engagement.*

    Primary ~ {40 Points} .... _____

    1. Money Makers   _____

    2. SAM Actions   _____

    Secondary ~ {20 Points}   .... _____

    1. R & D   _____

    2. Networking   _____

    Bizyness ~ {10 Points}   .... _____

    1. PATTs   _____

    2. G & A   _____

Nutrition—*Controlling our own destiny.*

    Calories ~ {7 Points} .... _____

    Nutraceuticals ~ {1 Point} .... _____

    Hydration ~ {2 Points} .... _____

Exercise—*Do it! Do it right! Do it right now!*

    Physical ~ {7 Points}   _____ _____

    Breathing ~ {3 Points} .... _____

Reading—*The man who reads is the man who leads.*   {5 Points} .... _____

    1. Spirituality ~ {2 Points}   _____

    2. Business ~ {2 Points}   _____

    3. Recreation ~ {1 Point}   _____

M.B.O.—*My future depends on many things, but mostly on me.*   {3 Points} .... _____

    1. Score ~ {1 Point}   _____

    2. Plan ~ {1 Point}   _____

    3. Save ~ {1 Point}   _____

Relationships—*"SMILE"*   {1 Point} .... _____

Personal Time—*"R & R 4me"*   {1 Point} .... _____

Selling = 4 to 5 hours a day

Total Daily Points ...   *"If not me, who?"*   .... **_____**

Target for the Day ...   *"If not now, when?*   .... **_____**

My Can-Do Chant
"I can ... I will ... I'm good!"

Food Item	Cals	Fats	Choles	Carbs	Pros
Targets	*2000*	*80*	*300*	*250*	*90*
Totals					

If you <u>score</u>, you do <u>less</u> & <u>more!</u>

Quote of the Day

"Make the most of yourself, for that is all there is of you."
Ralph Waldo Emerson

Water

8	24	40	56	72	88	104	120
0	16	32	48	64	80	96	112	128

Breathing

AM		Noon		PM	

Goals

Weight:	
Exercise:	
Score:	

"If it's to be, it's up to me!"

Power Performance

Daily Success Scorecard

Week: _____5_____   Day: _____1_____   Date: _____

Be Your Own Best Boss

Business Matters—*Nothing happens without engagement.*

Primary ~ {40 Points} .... _____
1. Money Makers _____
2. SAM Actions _____
Secondary ~ {20 Points} .... _____
1. R & D _____
2. Networking _____
Bizyness ~ {10 Points} .... _____
1. PATTs _____
2. G & A _____

Nutrition—*Controlling our own destiny.*

Calories ~ {7 Points}... _____
Nutraceuticals ~ {1 Point}..................................... _____
Hydration ~ {2 Points} .... _____

Exercise—*Do it! Do it right! Do it right now!*

Physical ~ {7 Points} _____ _____
Breathing ~ {3 Points} .... _____

Reading—*The man who reads is the man who leads.*   {5 Points} .... _____
1. Spirituality ~ {2 Points} _____
2. Business ~ {2 Points} _____
3. Recreation ~ {1 Point} _____

M.B.O.—*My future depends on many things, but mostly on me.*   {3 Points} .... _____
1. Score ~ {1 Point} _____
2. Plan ~ {1 Point} _____
3. Save ~ {1 Point} _____

Relationships—*"SMILE"*   {1 Point}........ _____
Personal Time—*"R & R 4me"*   {1 Point}........ _____

Selling = 4 to 5 hours a day

Total Daily Points ...   *"If not me, who?"* .... _____
Target for the Day ...   *"If not now, when?* .... _____

My Can-Do Chant
"I can ... I will ... I'm good!"

FOOD ITEM	CALS	FATS	CHOLES	CARBS	PROS
Targets	*2000*	*80*	*300*	*250*	*90*
TOTALS					

If you <u>score</u>, you do <u>less</u> & <u>more</u>!

QUOTE OF THE DAY

"Success is a ladder you cannot climb with your hands in your pockets."
American proverb

WATER

8	24	40	56	72	88	104	120
0	16	32	48	64	80	96	112	128

BREATHING

AM	Noon	PM

GOALS

WEIGHT:	_____
EXERCISE:	_____
SCORE:	_____

"If it's to be, it's up to me!"

Power Performance
Daily Success Scorecard

Week: _____ 5 _____ Day: _____ 2 _____ Date: _____

Be Your Own Best Boss

Business Matters—*Nothing happens without engagement.*

    Primary ~ {40 Points} .... _____

    1. Money Makers   _____

    2. SAM Actions   _____

    Secondary ~ {20 Points}   .... _____

    1. R & D   _____

    2. Networking   _____

    Bizyness ~ {10 Points}   .... _____

    1. PATTs   _____

    2. G & A   _____

Nutrition—*Controlling our own destiny.*

    Calories ~ {7 Points}... _____

    Nutraceuticals ~ {1 Point}... _____

    Hydration ~ {2 Points} .... _____

Exercise—*Do it! Do it right! Do it right now!*

    Physical ~ {7 Points}   _____ _____

    Breathing ~ {3 Points} .... _____

Reading—*The man who reads is the man who leads.*   {5 Points} .... _____

    1. Spirituality ~ {2 Points}   _____

    2. Business ~ {2 Points}   _____

    3. Recreation ~ {1 Point}   _____

M.B.O.—*My future depends on many things, but mostly on me.*   {3 Points} .... _____

    1. Score ~ {1 Point}   _____

    2. Plan ~ {1 Point}   _____

    3. Save ~ {1 Point}   _____

Relationships—*"SMILE"*   {1 Point}......... _____

Personal Time—*"R & R 4me"*   {1 Point}......... _____

Selling = 4 to 5 hours a day

Total Daily Points ...   *"If not me, who?"*   .... _____

Target for the Day ...   *"If not now, when?*"   .... _____

My Can-Do Chant
"I can ... I will ... I'm good!"

Food Item	Cals	Fats	Choles	Carbs	Pros
Targets	*2000*	*80*	*300*	*250*	*90*
Totals					

If you <u>score</u>, you do <u>less</u> & <u>more!</u>

Quote of the Day

"When it is obvious that the goals cannot be reached, don't adjust the goals, adjust the action steps."
Confucius

Water

8	24	40	56	72	88	104	120
0	16	32	48	64	80	96	112	128

Breathing

AM		Noon		PM	

Goals

WEIGHT:	_____
EXERCISE:	_____
SCORE:	_____

"If it's to be, it's up to me!"

Power Performance
Daily Success Scorecard

Week: ___5___   Day: ___3___   Date: _____

Be Your Own Best Boss

Business Matters—*Nothing happens without engagement.*

Primary ~ {40 Points} .... _____
1. Money Makers   _____
2. SAM Actions   _____
Secondary ~ {20 Points}   .... _____
1. R & D   _____
2. Networking   _____
Bizyness ~ {10 Points}   .... _____
1. PATTs   _____
2. G & A   _____

Nutrition—*Controlling our own destiny.*

Calories ~ {7 Points}.. _____
Nutraceuticals ~ {1 Point}.................................... _____
Hydration ~ {2 Points} .... _____

Exercise—*Do it! Do it right! Do it right now!*

Physical ~ {7 Points}   _____ _____
Breathing ~ {3 Points} .... _____

Reading—*The man who reads is the man who leads.*   {5 Points} .... _____
1. Spirituality ~ {2 Points}   _____
2. Business ~ {2 Points}   _____
3. Recreation ~ {1 Point}   _____

M.B.O.—*My future depends on many things, but mostly on me.*   {3 Points} .... _____
1. Score ~ {1 Point}   _____
2. Plan ~ {1 Point}   _____
3. Save ~ {1 Point}   _____

Relationships—*"SMILE"*   {1 Point} .... _____

Personal Time—*"R & R 4me"*   {1 Point} .... _____

Selling = 4 to 5 hours a day

Total Daily Points ...   *"If not me, who?"*   .... _____

Target for the Day ...   *"If not now, when?*   .... _____

My Can-Do Chant
"I can … I will … I'm good!"

Food Item	Cals	Fats	Choles	Carbs	Pros
Targets	*2000*	*80*	*300*	*250*	*90*
Totals					

If you <u>score</u>, you do <u>less</u> & <u>more</u>!

Quote of the Day

"Being ignorant is not so much a shame, as being unwilling to learn."
Benjamin Franklin

Water

8	24	40	56	72	88	104	120
0 16	32	48	64	80	96	112	128

Breathing

	AM		Noon		PM	

Goals

Weight:	_____
Exercise:	_____
Score:	_____

"If it's to be, it's up to me!"

Power Performance

Daily Success Scorecard

Week: ___5___   Day: ___4___   Date: _____

Be Your Own Best Boss

Business Matters—*Nothing happens without engagement.*

    Primary ~ {40 Points} .... _____

    1. Money Makers _____

    2. SAM Actions _____

    Secondary ~ {20 Points} .... _____

    1. R & D _____

    2. Networking _____

    Bizyness ~ {10 Points} .... _____

    1. PATTs _____

    2. G & A _____

Nutrition—*Controlling our own destiny.*

    Calories ~ {7 Points} .... _____

    Nutraceuticals ~ {1 Point} .... _____

    Hydration ~ {2 Points} .... _____

Exercise—*Do it! Do it right! Do it right now!*

    Physical ~ {7 Points} _____ _____

    Breathing ~ {3 Points} .... _____

Reading—*The man who reads is the man who leads.*   {5 Points} .... _____

    1. Spirituality ~ {2 Points} _____

    2. Business ~ {2 Points} _____

    3. Recreation ~ {1 Point} _____

M.B.O.—*My future depends on many things, but mostly on me.*   {3 Points} .... _____

    1. Score ~ {1 Point} _____

    2. Plan ~ {1 Point} _____

    3. Save ~ {1 Point} _____

Relationships—*"SMILE"*   {1 Point} .... _____

Personal Time—*"R & R 4me"*   {1 Point} .... _____

Selling = 4 to 5 hours a day

Total Daily Points ...   *"If not me, who?"*   .... _____

Target for the Day ...   *"If not now, when?*   .... _____

MY CAN-DO CHANT
"I can ... I will ... I'm good!"

FOOD ITEM	CALS	FATS	CHOLES	CARBS	PROS
Targets	*2000*	*80*	*300*	*250*	*90*
TOTALS					

If you <u>score</u>, you do <u>less</u> & <u>more</u>!

QUOTE OF THE DAY

"Defeat is not the worst of failures. Not to have tried is the true failure."
George E. Woodbury

WATER

8	24	40	56	72	88	104	120
0	16	32	48	64	80	96	112	128

BREATHING

AM		Noon		PM	

GOALS

WEIGHT: _____
EXERCISE: _____
SCORE: _____

"If it's to be, it's up to me!"

Power Performance
Daily Success Scorecard

Week: _____ 5 _____ Day: _____ 5 _____ Date: _____

Be Your Own Best Boss

Business Matters—*Nothing happens without engagement.*

    Primary ~ {40 Points} .... _____

    1. Money Makers   _____

    2. SAM Actions   _____

    Secondary ~ {20 Points}   .... _____

    1. R & D   _____

    2. Networking   _____

    Bizyness ~ {10 Points}   .... _____

    1. PATTs   _____

    2. G & A   _____

Nutrition—*Controlling our own destiny.*

    Calories ~ {7 Points}... _____

    Nutraceuticals ~ {1 Point}................................... _____

    Hydration ~ {2 Points} .... _____

Exercise—*Do it! Do it right! Do it right now!*

    Physical ~ {7 Points}   _____ _____

    Breathing ~ {3 Points} .... _____

Reading—*The man who reads is the man who leads.*   {5 Points} .... _____

    1. Spirituality ~ {2 Points}   _____

    2. Business ~ {2 Points}   _____

    3. Recreation ~ {1 Point}   _____

M.B.O.—*My future depends on many things, but mostly on me.*   {3 Points} .... _____

    1. Score ~ {1 Point}   _____

    2. Plan ~ {1 Point}   _____

    3. Save ~ {1 Point}   _____

Relationships—*"SMILE"*   {1 Point} .... _____

Personal Time—*"R & R 4me"*   {1 Point} .... _____

Selling = 4 to 5 hours a day

Total Daily Points ...   *"If not me, who?"*   .... _____

Target for the Day ...   *"If not now, when?"*   .... _____

My Can-Do Chant
"I can ... I will ... I'm good!"

Food Item	Cals	Fats	Choles	Carbs	Pros
Targets	*2000*	*80*	*300*	*250*	*90*
Totals					

If you <u>score</u>, you do <u>less</u> & <u>more!</u>

Quote of the Day

"All human beings should try to learn before they die what
they are running from, and to, and why."
James Thurber

Water

8	24	40	56	72	88	104	120
0 16	32	48	64	80	96	112	128

Breathing

AM		Noon		PM	

Goals

WEIGHT: _____
EXERCISE: _____
SCORE: _____

"If it's to be, it's up to me!"

Power Performance

Daily Success Scorecard

Week: _____ 5 _____ Day: _____ 6 _____ Date: _____

Be Your Own Best Boss

Business Matters—*Nothing happens without engagement.*

Primary ~ {40 Points} .... _____

1. Money Makers _____

2. SAM Actions _____

Secondary ~ {20 Points} .... _____

1. R & D _____

2. Networking _____

Bizyness ~ {10 Points} .... _____

1. PATTs _____

2. G & A _____

Nutrition—*Controlling our own destiny.*

Calories ~ {7 Points}... _____

Nutraceuticals ~ {1 Point}.. _____

Hydration ~ {2 Points} .... _____

Exercise—*Do it! Do it right! Do it right now!*

Physical ~ {7 Points} _____ _____

Breathing ~ {3 Points} .... _____

Reading—*The man who reads is the man who leads.*   {5 Points} .... _____

1. Spirituality ~ {2 Points} _____

2. Business ~ {2 Points} _____

3. Recreation ~ {1 Point} _____

M.B.O.—*My future depends on many things, but mostly on me.*   {3 Points} .... _____

1. Score ~ {1 Point} _____

2. Plan ~ {1 Point} _____

3. Save ~ {1 Point} _____

Relationships—*"SMILE"*   {1 Point} .... _____

Personal Time—*"R & R 4me"*   {1 Point} .... _____

Selling = 4 to 5 hours a day

Total Daily Points ...   *"If not me, who?"*   .... _____

Target for the Day ...   *"If not now, when?"*   .... _____

My Can-Do Chant
"I can ... I will ... I'm good!"

Food Item	Cals	Fats	Choles	Carbs	Pros
Targets	*2000*	*80*	*300*	*250*	*90*
Totals					

If you <u>score</u>, you do <u>less</u> & more!

Quote of the Day

"Vitality shows not only in the ability to persist, but in the ability to start over."
F. Scott Fitzgerald

Water

8	24	40	56	72	88	104	120
0	16	32	48	64	80	96	112	128

Breathing

AM		Noon		PM	

Goals

Weight:	
Exercise:	
Score:	

"If it's to be, it's up to me!"

Power Performance

Daily Success Scorecard

Week: ____5____ Day: ____7____ Date: _____

Be Your Own Best Boss

Business Matters—*Nothing happens without engagement.*

Primary ~ {40 Points} .... _____

   1. Money Makers   _____

   2. SAM Actions   _____

Secondary ~ {20 Points}   .... _____

   1. R & D   _____

   2. Networking   _____

Bizyness ~ {10 Points}   .... _____

   1. PATTs   _____

   2. G & A   _____

Nutrition—*Controlling our own destiny.*

Calories ~ {7 Points}.. _____

Nutraceuticals ~ {1 Point} .... _____

Hydration ~ {2 Points} .... _____

Exercise—*Do it! Do it right! Do it right now!*

Physical ~ {7 Points}   _____ _____

Breathing ~ {3 Points} .... _____

Reading—*The man who reads is the man who leads.*   {5 Points} .... _____

   1. Spirituality ~ {2 Points}   _____

   2. Business ~ {2 Points}   _____

   3. Recreation ~ {1 Point}   _____

M.B.O.—*My future depends on many things, but mostly on me.*   {3 Points} .... _____

   1. Score ~ {1 Point}   _____

   2. Plan ~ {1 Point}   _____

   3. Save ~ {1 Point}   _____

Relationships—*"SMILE"*   {1 Point}......... _____

Personal Time—*"R & R 4me"*   {1 Point}......... _____

Selling = 4 to 5 hours a day

Total Daily Points ... *"If not me, who?"*   .... _____

Target for the Day ... *"If not now, when?"*   .... _____

My Can-Do Chant
"I can ... I will ... I'm good!"

Food Item	Cals	Fats	Choles	Carbs	Pros
Targets	*2000*	*80*	*300*	*250*	*90*
Totals					

If you <u>score</u>, you do <u>less</u> & <u>more</u>!

Quote of the Day

"Failure is the opportunity to begin again, more intelligently."
Henry Ford

Water

8	24	40	56	72	88	104	120
0	16	32	48	64	80	96	112	128

Breathing

AM		Noon		PM	

Goals

WEIGHT:	_____
EXERCISE:	_____
SCORE:	_____

"If it's to be, it's up to me!"

Personal
Power Performance
Daily Success Scorecard

Week: ___6___   Day: ___1___   Date: _____

Be Your Own Best Boss

Business Matters—*Nothing happens without engagement.*

Primary ~ {40 Points} .... _____

  1. Money Makers   _____

  2. SAM Actions   _____

Secondary ~ {20 Points}   .... _____

  1. R & D   _____

  2. Networking   _____

Bizyness ~ {10 Points}   .... _____

  1. PATTs   _____

  2. G & A   _____

Nutrition—*Controlling our own destiny.*

Calories ~ {7 Points} .... _____

Nutraceuticals ~ {1 Point} .... _____

Hydration ~ {2 Points} .... _____

Exercise—*Do it! Do it right! Do it right now!*

Physical ~ {7 Points}   _____ _____

Breathing ~ {3 Points} .... _____

Reading—*The man who reads is the man who leads.*   {5 Points} .... _____

  1. Spirituality ~ {2 Points}   _____

  2. Business ~ {2 Points}   _____

  3. Recreation ~ {1 Point}   _____

M.B.O.—*My future depends on many things, but mostly on me.*   {3 Points} .... _____

  1. Score ~ {1 Point}   _____

  2. Plan ~ {1 Point}   _____

  3. Save ~ {1 Point}   _____

Relationships—*"SMILE"*   {1 Point} .... _____

Personal Time—*"R & R 4me"*   {1 Point} .... _____

Selling = 4 to 5 hours a day

Total Daily Points ... *"If not me, who?"* .... _____

Target for the Day ... *"If not now, when?*" .... _____

71

MY CAN-DO CHANT
"I can ... I will ... I'm good!"

FOOD ITEM	CALS	FATS	CHOLES	CARBS	PROS
Targets	*2000*	*80*	*300*	*250*	*90*
TOTALS					

If you <u>score</u>, you do <u>less</u> & <u>more</u>!

QUOTE OF THE DAY

"It is not the strongest of the species that survive, nor the most intelligent, but the most responsive to change."
Charles Darwin

WATER

8	24	40	56	72	88	104	120
0	16	32	48	64	80	96	112	128

BREATHING

AM		Noon		PM	

GOALS

WEIGHT: _____
EXERCISE: _____
SCORE: _____

"If it's to be, it's up to me!"

Personal
Power Performance
Daily Success Scorecard

Week: ___6___ Day: ___2___ Date: _____

Be Your Own Best Boss

Business Matters—*Nothing happens without engagement.*

Primary ~ {40 Points} .... _____

1. Money Makers _____

2. SAM Actions _____

Secondary ~ {20 Points} .... _____

1. R & D _____

2. Networking _____

Bizyness ~ {10 Points} .... _____

1. PATTs _____

2. G & A _____

Nutrition—*Controlling our own destiny.*

Calories ~ {7 Points}............................ _____

Nutraceuticals ~ {1 Point}............................ _____

Hydration ~ {2 Points} .... _____

Exercise—*Do it! Do it right! Do it right now!*

Physical ~ {7 Points} _____ _____

Breathing ~ {3 Points} .... _____

Reading—*The man who reads is the man who leads.* {5 Points} .... _____

1. Spirituality ~ {2 Points} _____

2. Business ~ {2 Points} _____

3. Recreation ~ {1 Point} _____

M.B.O.—*My future depends on many things, but mostly on me.* {3 Points} .... _____

1. Score ~ {1 Point} _____

2. Plan ~ {1 Point} _____

3. Save ~ {1 Point} _____

Relationships—*"SMILE"* {1 Point} .... _____

Personal Time—*"R & R 4me"* {1 Point} .... _____

Selling = 4 to 5 hours a day

Total Daily Points ... *"If not me, who?"* .... _____

Target for the Day ... *"If not now, when?* .... _____

MY CAN-DO CHANT
"I can ... I will ... I'm good!"

FOOD ITEM	CALS	FATS	CHOLES	CARBS	PROS
Targets	*2000*	*80*	*300*	*250*	*90*
TOTALS					

If you <u>score</u>, you do <u>less</u> & <u>more</u>!

QUOTE OF THE DAY

"Big jobs usually go to the men who prove their ability to outgrow small ones."
Theodore Roosevelt

WATER

8	24	40	56	72	88	104	120
0	16	32	48	64	80	96	112	128

BREATHING

AM		Noon		PM	

GOALS

WEIGHT: _____
EXERCISE: _____
SCORE: _____

"If it's to be, it's up to me!"

Power Performance
Daily Success Scorecard

Week: _____6_____   Day: _____3_____   Date: _____

Be Your Own Best Boss

Business Matters—*Nothing happens without engagement.*

    Primary ~ {40 Points} .... _____

    1. Money Makers   _____

    2. SAM Actions   _____

    Secondary ~ {20 Points}   .... _____

    1. R & D   _____

    2. Networking   _____

    Bizyness ~ {10 Points}   .... _____

    1. PATTs   _____

    2. G & A   _____

Nutrition—*Controlling our own destiny.*

    Calories ~ {7 Points}.. _____

    Nutraceuticals ~ {1 Point}.. _____

    Hydration ~ {2 Points} .... _____

Exercise—*Do it! Do it right! Do it right now!*

    Physical ~ {7 Points}   _____ _____

    Breathing ~ {3 Points} .... _____

Reading—*The man who reads is the man who leads.*   {5 Points} .... _____

    1. Spirituality ~ {2 Points}   _____

    2. Business ~ {2 Points}   _____

    3. Recreation ~ {1 Point}   _____

M.B.O.—*My future depends on many things, but mostly on me.*   {3 Points} .... _____

    1. Score ~ {1 Point}   _____

    2. Plan ~ {1 Point}   _____

    3. Save ~ {1 Point}   _____

Relationships—*"SMILE"*   {1 Point} .... _____

Personal Time—*"R & R 4me"*   {1 Point} .... _____

Selling = 4 to 5 hours a day

Total Daily Points ...   *"If not me, who?"*   .... _____

Target for the Day ...   *"If not now, when?*   .... _____

MY CAN-DO CHANT
"I can ... I will ... I'm good!"

FOOD ITEM	CALS	FATS	CHOLES	CARBS	PROS
Targets	*2000*	*80*	*300*	*250*	*90*
TOTALS					

If you <u>score</u>, you do <u>less</u> & <u>more</u>!

QUOTE OF THE DAY

"Time is what we want most, but what we use worst."
William Penn

WATER

8	24	40	56	72	88	104	120
0	16	32	48	64	80	96	112	128

BREATHING

AM		Noon		PM	

GOALS

WEIGHT: _____
EXERCISE: _____
SCORE: _____

"If it's to be, it's up to me!"

Power Performance

Daily Success Scorecard

Week: ___6___   Day: ___4___   Date: _____

Be Your Own Best Boss

Business Matters—*Nothing happens without engagement.*

    Primary ~ {40 Points} .... _____

    1. Money Makers   _____

    2. SAM Actions   _____

    Secondary ~ {20 Points}   .... _____

    1. R & D   _____

    2. Networking   _____

    Bizyness ~ {10 Points}   .... _____

    1. PATTs   _____

    2. G & A   _____

Nutrition—*Controlling our own destiny.*

    Calories ~ {7 Points} .... _____

    Nutraceuticals ~ {1 Point} .... _____

    Hydration ~ {2 Points} .... _____

Exercise—*Do it! Do it right! Do it right now!*

    Physical ~ {7 Points}   _____ _____

    Breathing ~ {3 Points} .... _____

Reading—*The man who reads is the man who leads.*   {5 Points} .... _____

    1. Spirituality ~ {2 Points}   _____

    2. Business ~ {2 Points}   _____

    3. Recreation ~ {1 Point}   _____

M.B.O.—*My future depends on many things, but mostly on me.*   {3 Points} .... _____

    1. Score ~ {1 Point}   _____

    2. Plan ~ {1 Point}   _____

    3. Save ~ {1 Point}   _____

Relationships—*"SMILE"*   {1 Point} .... _____

Personal Time—*"R & R 4me"*   {1 Point} .... _____

Selling = 4 to 5 hours a day

Total Daily Points ...   *"If not me, who?"*   .... _____

Target for the Day ...   *"If not now, when?"*   .... _____

MY CAN-DO CHANT
"I can ... I will ... I'm good!"

FOOD ITEM	CALS	FATS	CHOLES	CARBS	PROS
Targets	*2000*	*80*	*300*	*250*	*90*
TOTALS					

If you <u>score</u>, you do <u>less</u> & <u>more</u>!

QUOTE OF THE DAY

"The most pathetic person in the world is someone who has sight but has no vision."
Helen Keller

WATER

8	24	40	56	72	88	104	120
0 16	32	48	64	80	96	112	128

BREATHING

AM		Noon		PM	

GOALS

WEIGHT:	_____
EXERCISE:	_____
SCORE:	_____

"If it's to be, it's up to me!"

Power Performance

Daily Success Scorecard

Week: ____6____   Day: ____5____   Date: _____

Be Your Own Best Boss

Business Matters—*Nothing happens without engagement.*

Primary ~ {40 Points} .... _____

   1. Money Makers   _____

   2. SAM Actions   _____

Secondary ~ {20 Points}   .... _____

   1. R & D   _____

   2. Networking   _____

Bizyness ~ {10 Points}   .... _____

   1. PATTs   _____

   2. G & A   _____

Nutrition—*Controlling our own destiny.*

Calories ~ {7 Points} .... _____

Nutraceuticals ~ {1 Point} .... _____

Hydration ~ {2 Points} .... _____

Exercise—*Do it! Do it right! Do it right now!*

Physical ~ {7 Points}   _____ _____

Breathing ~ {3 Points} .... _____

Reading—*The man who reads is the man who leads.*   {5 Points} .... _____

   1. Spirituality ~ {2 Points}   _____

   2. Business ~ {2 Points}   _____

   3. Recreation ~ {1 Point}   _____

_M.B.O._—*My future depends on many things, but mostly on me.*   {3 Points} .... _____

   1. Score ~ {1 Point}   _____

   2. Plan ~ {1 Point}   _____

   3. Save ~ {1 Point}   _____

Relationships—*"SMILE"*   {1 Point} .... _____

Personal Time—*"R & R 4me"*   {1 Point} .... _____

Selling = 4 to 5 hours a day

Total Daily Points ...   *"If not me, who?"*   .... **_____**

Target for the Day ...   *"If not now, when?*   .... **_____**

My Can-Do Chant
"I can ... I will ... I'm good!"

Food Item	Cals	Fats	Choles	Carbs	Pros
Targets	*2000*	*80*	*300*	*250*	*90*
Totals					

If you <u>score</u>, you do <u>less</u> & <u>more</u>!

Quote of the Day

"Procrastination is something best put off until tomorrow."
Gerald Vaughan

Water

8	24	40	56	72	88	104	120
0	16	32	48	64	80	96	112	128

Breathing

AM		Noon		PM	

Goals

Weight: _____
Exercise: _____
Score: _____

"If it's to be, it's up to me!"

80

Personal
Power Performance
Daily Success Scorecard

Week: ___6___   Day: ___6___   Date: _____

Be Your Own Best Boss

Business Matters—*Nothing happens without engagement.*

    Primary ~ {40 Points} .... _____

    1. Money Makers   _____

    2. SAM Actions   _____

    Secondary ~ {20 Points}   .... _____

    1. R & D   _____

    2. Networking   _____

    Bizyness ~ {10 Points}   .... _____

    1. PATTs   _____

    2. G & A   _____

Nutrition—*Controlling our own destiny.*

    Calories ~ {7 Points} .... _____

    Nutraceuticals ~ {1 Point} .... _____

    Hydration ~ {2 Points} .... _____

Exercise—*Do it! Do it right! Do it right now!*

    Physical ~ {7 Points}   _____ _____

    Breathing ~ {3 Points} .... _____

Reading—*The man who reads is the man who leads.*   {5 Points} .... _____

    1. Spirituality ~ {2 Points}   _____

    2. Business ~ {2 Points}   _____

    3. Recreation ~ {1 Point}   _____

M.B.O.—*My future depends on many things, but mostly on me.*   {3 Points} .... _____

    1. Score ~ {1 Point}   _____

    2. Plan ~ {1 Point}   _____

    3. Save ~ {1 Point}   _____

Relationships—*"SMILE"*   {1 Point} .... _____

Personal Time—*"R & R 4me"*   {1 Point} .... _____

Selling = 4 to 5 hours a day

Total Daily Points ...   *"If not me, who?"*   .... _____

Target for the Day ...   *"If not now, when?"*   .... _____

MY CAN-DO CHANT
"I can … I will … I'm good!"

FOOD ITEM	CALS	FATS	CHOLES	CARBS	PROS
Targets	*2000*	*80*	*300*	*250*	*90*
TOTALS					

If you <u>score</u>, you do <u>less</u> & <u>more</u>!

QUOTE OF THE DAY
"The only time when something is ever half-empty is when it concerns how you truly live your whole life. Live it well and it is always full."
Richard Possett

WATER

8	24	40	56	72	88	104	120
0	16	32	48	64	80	96	112	128

BREATHING

AM		Noon		PM	

GOALS

WEIGHT: _____
EXERCISE: _____
SCORE: _____

"If it's to be, it's up to me!"

Personal
Power Performance
Daily Success Scorecard

Week: ___6___   Day: ___7___   Date: _____

Be Your Own Best Boss

Business Matters—*Nothing happens without engagement.*

Primary ~ {40 Points} .... ____

  1. Money Makers   _____

  2. SAM Actions   _____

Secondary ~ {20 Points}   .... ____

  1. R & D   _____

  2. Networking   _____

Bizyness ~ {10 Points}   .... ____

  1. PATTs   _____

  2. G & A   _____

Nutrition—*Controlling our own destiny.*

Calories ~ {7 Points} .... ____

Nutraceuticals ~ {1 Point} .... ____

Hydration ~ {2 Points} .... ____

Exercise—*Do it! Do it right! Do it right now!*

Physical ~ {7 Points}   _____ ____

Breathing ~ {3 Points} .... ____

Reading—*The man who reads is the man who leads.*   {5 Points} .... ____

  1. Spirituality ~ {2 Points}   _____

  2. Business ~ {2 Points}   _____

  3. Recreation ~ {1 Point}   _____

M.B.O.—*My future depends on many things, but mostly on me.*   {3 Points} .... ____

  1. Score ~ {1 Point}   _____

  2. Plan ~ {1 Point}   _____

  3. Save ~ {1 Point}   _____

Relationships—*"SMILE"*   {1 Point} .... ____

Personal Time—*"R & R 4me"*   {1 Point} .... ____

Selling = 4 to 5 hours a day

Total Daily Points ... *"If not me, who?"* .... ____

Target for the Day ... *"If not now, when?* .... ____

83

My Can-Do Chant
"I can ... I will ... I'm good!"

FOOD ITEM	CALS	FATS	CHOLES	CARBS	PROS
Targets	*2000*	*80*	*300*	*250*	*90*
TOTALS					

If you <u>score</u>, you do <u>less</u> & <u>more</u>!

QUOTE OF THE DAY

"Today is a new day. You will get out of it just what you put into it ..."
Mary Pickford

WATER

| 0 | 8 | 16 | 24 | 32 | 40 | 48 | 56 | 64 | 72 | 80 | 88 | 96 | 104 | 112 | 120 | 128 |

BREATHING

AM		Noon		PM	

GOALS

WEIGHT: _____
EXERCISE: _____
SCORE: _____

"If it's to be, it's up to me!"

Personal
Power Performance
Daily Success Scorecard

Week: _____7_____ Day: _____1_____ Date: _____

Be Your Own Best Boss

Business Matters—*Nothing happens without engagement.*

Primary ~ {40 Points} .... _____

  1. Money Makers   _____

  2. SAM Actions   _____

Secondary ~ {20 Points}   .... _____

  1. R & D   _____

  2. Networking   _____

Bizyness ~ {10 Points}   .... _____

  1. PATTs   _____

  2. G & A   _____

Nutrition—*Controlling our own destiny.*

Calories ~ {7 Points}.. _____

Nutraceuticals ~ {1 Point}.. _____

Hydration ~ {2 Points} .... _____

Exercise—*Do it! Do it right! Do it right now!*

Physical ~ {7 Points}   _____

Breathing ~ {3 Points} .... _____

Reading—*The man who reads is the man who leads.*   {5 Points} .... _____

  1. Spirituality ~ {2 Points}   _____

  2. Business ~ {2 Points}   _____

  3. Recreation ~ {1 Point}   _____

M.B.O.—*My future depends on many things, but mostly on me.*   {3 Points} .... _____

  1. Score ~ {1 Point}   _____

  2. Plan ~ {1 Point}   _____

  3. Save ~ {1 Point}   _____

Relationships—*"SMILE"*   {1 Point} .... _____

Personal Time—*"R & R 4me"*   {1 Point} .... _____

Selling = 4 to 5 hours a day

Total Daily Points ...   *"If not me, who?"* .... _____

Target for the Day ...   *"If not now, when?* .... _____

My Can-Do Chant
"I can ... I will ... I'm good!"

Food Item	Cals	Fats	Choles	Carbs	Pros
Targets	*2000*	*80*	*300*	*250*	*90*
Totals					

If you <u>score</u>, you do <u>less</u> & <u>more</u>!

Quote of the Day

"In the middle of difficulty lies opportunity."
Albert Einstein

Water

8	24	40	56	72	88	104	120
0	16	32	48	64	80	96	112	128

Breathing

AM		Noon		PM	

Goals

Weight:	
Exercise:	
Score:	

"If it's to be, it's up to me!"

Power Performance
Daily Success Scorecard

Week: _____7_____ Day: _____2_____ Date: _____

Be Your Own Best Boss

Business Matters—*Nothing happens without engagement.*

Primary ~ {40 Points} .... _____
1. Money Makers _____
2. SAM Actions _____
Secondary ~ {20 Points} .... _____
1. R & D _____
2. Networking _____
Bizyness ~ {10 Points} .... _____
1. PATTs _____
2. G & A _____

Nutrition—*Controlling our own destiny.*

Calories ~ {7 Points}...
Nutraceuticals ~ {1 Point}.. _____
Hydration ~ {2 Points} .... _____

Exercise—*Do it! Do it right! Do it right now!*

Physical ~ {7 Points} _____ _____
Breathing ~ {3 Points} ....

Reading—*The man who reads is the man who leads.*   {5 Points} .... _____
1. Spirituality ~ {2 Points} _____
2. Business ~ {2 Points} _____
3. Recreation ~ {1 Point} _____

M.B.O.—*My future depends on many things, but mostly on me.* {3 Points} .... _____
1. Score ~ {1 Point} _____
2. Plan ~ {1 Point} _____
3. Save ~ {1 Point} _____

Relationships—*"SMILE"*   {1 Point} .... _____
Personal Time—*"R & R 4me"*   {1 Point} .... _____

Selling = 4 to 5 hours a day

Total Daily Points ...   *"If not me, who?"*   .... _____
Target for the Day ...   *"If not now, when?*   .... _____

MY CAN-DO CHANT
"I can ... I will ... I'm good!"

FOOD ITEM	CALS	FATS	CHOLES	CARBS	PROS
Targets	*2000*	*80*	*300*	*250*	*90*
TOTALS					

If you <u>score</u>, you do <u>less</u> & <u>more</u>!

QUOTE OF THE DAY

"Activity is contagious."
Ralph Waldo Emerson

WATER

8	24	40	56	72	88	104	120
0	16	32	48	64	80	96	112	128

BREATHING

AM		Noon		PM	

GOALS

WEIGHT: _____
EXERCISE: _____
SCORE: _____

"If it's to be, it's up to me!"

Power Performance

Daily Success Scorecard

Week: _____ 7 _____ Day: _____ 3 _____ Date: _____

Be Your Own Best Boss

Business Matters—*Nothing happens without engagement.*

Primary ~ {40 Points} .... _____
1. Money Makers   _____
2. SAM Actions   _____
Secondary ~ {20 Points}   .... _____
1. R & D   _____
2. Networking   _____
Bizyness ~ {10 Points}   .... _____
1. PATTs   _____
2. G & A   _____

Nutrition—*Controlling our own destiny.*

Calories ~ {7 Points}...
Nutraceuticals ~ {1 Point}... _____
Hydration ~ {2 Points} ....

Exercise—*Do it! Do it right! Do it right now!*

Physical ~ {7 Points}   _____ _____
Breathing ~ {3 Points} ....

Reading—*The man who reads is the man who leads.*   {5 Points} .... _____
1. Spirituality ~ {2 Points}   _____
2. Business ~ {2 Points}   _____
3. Recreation ~ {1 Point}   _____

M.B.O.—*My future depends on many things, but mostly on me.*   {3 Points} .... _____
1. Score ~ {1 Point}   _____
2. Plan ~ {1 Point}   _____
3. Save ~ {1 Point}   _____

Relationships—*"SMILE"*   {1 Point} .... _____
Personal Time—*"R & R 4me"*   {1 Point} .... _____

Selling = 4 to 5 hours a day

Total Daily Points ...   *"If not me, who?"*   .... _____
Target for the Day ...   *"If not now, when?*   .... _____

My Can-Do Chant
"I can ... I will ... I'm good!"

Food Item	Cals	Fats	Choles	Carbs	Pros
Targets	*2000*	*80*	*300*	*250*	*90*
Totals					

If you <u>score</u>, you do <u>less</u> & <u>more</u>!

Quote of the Day

"The key to success is for you to make a habit throughout your life of doing the things you fear."
Vincent Van Gogh

Water

8	24	40	56	72	88	104	120
0	16	32	48	64	80	96	112	128

Breathing

AM		Noon		PM	

Goals

Weight:	_____
Exercise:	_____
Score:	_____

"If it's to be, it's up to me!"

Power Performance

Daily Success Scorecard

Week: _____ 7 _____   Day: _____ 4 _____   Date: _____

Be Your Own Best Boss

Business Matters—*Nothing happens without engagement.*

Primary ~ {40 Points} .... _____
1. Money Makers _____
2. SAM Actions _____

Secondary ~ {20 Points}   .... _____
1. R & D _____
2. Networking _____

Bizyness ~ {10 Points}   .... _____
1. PATTs _____
2. G & A _____

Nutrition—*Controlling our own destiny.*

Calories ~ {7 Points}... _____
Nutraceuticals ~ {1 Point}.................................. _____
Hydration ~ {2 Points} .... _____

Exercise—*Do it! Do it right! Do it right now!*

Physical ~ {7 Points} _____ _____
Breathing ~ {3 Points} .... _____

Reading—*The man who reads is the man who leads.*   {5 Points} .... _____
1. Spirituality ~ {2 Points} _____
2. Business ~ {2 Points} _____
3. Recreation ~ {1 Point} _____

M.B.O.—*My future depends on many things, but mostly on me.*   {3 Points} .... _____
1. Score ~ {1 Point} _____
2. Plan ~ {1 Point} _____
3. Save ~ {1 Point} _____

Relationships—*"SMILE"*   {1 Point}......... _____

Personal Time—*"R & R 4me"*   {1 Point}......... _____

Selling = 4 to 5 hours a day

Total Daily Points ...   *"If not me, who?"*   .... _____

Target for the Day ...   *"If not now, when?*   .... _____

My Can-Do Chant
"I can ... I will ... I'm good!"

Food Item	Cals	Fats	Choles	Carbs	Pros
Targets	*2000*	*80*	*300*	*250*	*90*
Totals					

If you <u>score</u>, you do <u>less</u> & <u>more</u>!

Quote of the Day

"Strive for perfection in everything. Take the best that exists and make it better. If it doesn't exist, create it."
Henry Royce

Water

8	24	40	56	72	88	104	120
0	16	32	48	64	80	96	112	128

Breathing

AM		Noon		PM	

Goals

Weight:	_____
Exercise:	_____
Score:	_____

"If it's to be, it's up to me!"

Power Performance
Daily Success Scorecard

Week: _____7_____   Day: _____5_____   Date: _____

Be Your Own Best Boss

Business Matters—*Nothing happens without engagement.*

    Primary ~ {40 Points} .... _____

    1. Money Makers   _____

    2. SAM Actions   _____

    Secondary ~ {20 Points}   .... _____

    1. R & D   _____

    2. Networking   _____

    Bizyness ~ {10 Points}   .... _____

    1. PATTs   _____

    2. G & A   _____

Nutrition—*Controlling our own destiny.*

    Calories ~ {7 Points} .... _____

    Nutraceuticals ~ {1 Point} .... _____

    Hydration ~ {2 Points} .... _____

Exercise—*Do it! Do it right! Do it right now!*

    Physical ~ {7 Points}   _____ _____

    Breathing ~ {3 Points} .... _____

Reading—*The man who reads is the man who leads.*   {5 Points} .... _____

    1. Spirituality ~ {2 Points}   _____

    2. Business ~ {2 Points}   _____

    3. Recreation ~ {1 Point}   _____

M.B.O.—*My future depends on many things, but mostly on me.*   {3 Points} .... _____

    1. Score ~ {1 Point}   _____

    2. Plan ~ {1 Point}   _____

    3. Save ~ {1 Point}   _____

Relationships—*"SMILE"*   {1 Point} .... _____

Personal Time—*"R & R 4me"*   {1 Point} .... _____

Selling = 4 to 5 hours a day

Total Daily Points ...   *"If not me, who?"*   .... _____

Target for the Day ...   *"If not now, when?*   .... _____

My Can-Do Chant
"I can … I will … I'm good!"

FOOD ITEM	CALS	FATS	CHOLES	CARBS	PROS
Targets	*2000*	*80*	*300*	*250*	*90*
TOTALS					

If you <u>score</u>, you do <u>less</u> & <u>more</u>!

QUOTE OF THE DAY

"A common goal, well done, is better than a good intention."
POZ

WATER

8		24		40		56		72		88		104		120	
0	16		32		48		64		80		96		112		128

BREATHING

AM			Noon		PM	

GOALS

WEIGHT: _____
EXERCISE: _____
SCORE: _____

"If it's to be, it's up to me!"

Power Performance

Daily Success Scorecard

Week: **7** Day: **6** Date: _____

Be Your Own Best Boss

<u>Business Matters</u>—*Nothing happens without engagement.*

    Primary ~ {40 Points} .... _____

    1. Money Makers   _____

    2. SAM Actions   _____

    Secondary ~ {20 Points}   .... _____

    1. R & D   _____

    2. Networking   _____

    Bizyness ~ {10 Points}   .... _____

    1. PATTs   _____

    2. G & A   _____

<u>Nutrition</u>—*Controlling our own destiny.*

    Calories ~ {7 Points} .... _____

    Nutraceuticals ~ {1 Point} .... _____

    Hydration ~ {2 Points} .... _____

<u>Exercise</u>—*Do it! Do it right! Do it right now!*

    Physical ~ {7 Points}   _____ _____

    Breathing ~ {3 Points} .... _____

<u>Reading</u>—*The man who reads is the man who leads.*   {5 Points} .... _____

    1. Spirituality ~ {2 Points}   _____

    2. Business ~ {2 Points}   _____

    3. Recreation ~ {1 Point}   _____

<u>M.B.O.</u>—*My future depends on many things, but mostly on me.*   {3 Points} .... _____

    1. Score ~ {1 Point}   _____

    2. Plan ~ {1 Point}   _____

    3. Save ~ {1 Point}   _____

<u>Relationships</u>—*"SMILE"*   {1 Point} .... _____

<u>Personal Time</u>—*"R & R 4me"*   {1 Point} .... _____

Selling = 4 to 5 hours a day

Total Daily Points ...   **"If not me, who?"**   .... _____

Target for the Day ...   **"If not now, when?"**   .... _____

My Can-Do Chant
"I can ... I will ... I'm good!"

Food Item	Cals	Fats	Choles	Carbs	Pros
Targets	*2000*	*80*	*300*	*250*	*90*
Totals					

If you <u>score</u>, you do <u>less</u> & <u>more!</u>

Quote of the Day

"Never let the fear of striking out get in your way."
Babe Ruth

Water

8	24	40	56	72	88	104	120
0	16	32	48	64	80	96	112	128

Breathing

AM		Noon		PM	

Goals

WEIGHT: _____
EXERCISE: _____
SCORE: _____

"If it's to be, it's up to me!"

Power Performance
Daily Success Scorecard

Week: _____ 7 _____   Day: _____ 7 _____   Date: _____

Be Your Own Best Boss

Business Matters—*Nothing happens without engagement.*
    Primary ~ {40 Points} .... _____
    1. Money Makers   _____
    2. SAM Actions   _____
    Secondary ~ {20 Points}   .... _____
    1. R & D   _____
    2. Networking   _____
    Bizyness ~ {10 Points}   .... _____
    1. PATTs   _____
    2. G & A   _____

Nutrition—*Controlling our own destiny.*
    Calories ~ {7 Points} .... _____
    Nutraceuticals ~ {1 Point} .... _____
    Hydration ~ {2 Points} .... _____

Exercise—*Do it! Do it right! Do it right now!*
    Physical ~ {7 Points}   _____ _____
    Breathing ~ {3 Points} .... _____

Reading—*The man who reads is the man who leads.*   {5 Points} .... _____
    1. Spirituality ~ {2 Points}   _____
    2. Business ~ {2 Points}   _____
    3. Recreation ~ {1 Point}   _____

M.B.O.—*My future depends on many things, but mostly on me.*   {3 Points} .... _____
    1. Score ~ {1 Point}   _____
    2. Plan ~ {1 Point}   _____
    3. Save ~ {1 Point}   _____

Relationships—*"SMILE"*   {1 Point} .... _____
Personal Time—*"R & R 4me"*   {1 Point} .... _____

Selling = 4 to 5 hours a day

Total Daily Points ...   *"If not me, who?"*   .... _____
Target for the Day ...   *"If not now, when?*   .... _____

MY CAN-DO CHANT
"I can … I will … I'm good!"

FOOD ITEM	CALS	FATS	CHOLES	CARBS	PROS
Targets	*2000*	*80*	*300*	*250*	*90*
TOTALS					

If you <u>score</u>, you do <u>less</u> & <u>more</u>!

QUOTE OF THE DAY

"Anyone who has never made a mistake has never tried anything new."
Albert Einstein

WATER

8	24	40	56	72	88	104	120
0	16	32	48	64	80	96	112	128

BREATHING

AM		Noon		PM	

GOALS

WEIGHT: _____
EXERCISE: _____
SCORE: _____

"If it's to be, it's up to me!"

Power Performance

Week: ___8___   Day: ___1___   Date: _____

Be Your Own Best Boss

Business Matters—*Nothing happens without engagement.*

    Primary ~ {40 Points} .... _____

    1. Money Makers   _____

    2. SAM Actions   _____

    Secondary ~ {20 Points}   .... _____

    1. R & D   _____

    2. Networking   _____

    Bizyness ~ {10 Points}   .... _____

    1. PATTs   _____

    2. G & A   _____

Nutrition—*Controlling our own destiny.*

    Calories ~ {7 Points} .... _____

    Nutraceuticals ~ {1 Point} .... _____

    Hydration ~ {2 Points} .... _____

Exercise—*Do it! Do it right! Do it right now!*

    Physical ~ {7 Points}   _____

    Breathing ~ {3 Points} .... _____

Reading—*The man who reads is the man who leads.*   {5 Points} .... _____

    1. Spirituality ~ {2 Points}   _____

    2. Business ~ {2 Points}   _____

    3. Recreation ~ {1 Point}   _____

M.B.O.—*My future depends on many things, but mostly on me.*   {3 Points} .... _____

    1. Score ~ {1 Point}   _____

    2. Plan ~ {1 Point}   _____

    3. Save ~ {1 Point}   _____

Relationships—*"SMILE"*   {1 Point} .... _____

Personal Time—*"R & R 4me"*   {1 Point} .... _____

Selling = 4 to 5 hours a day

Total Daily Points ...   *"If not me, who?"*   .... _____

Target for the Day ...   *"If not now, when?*   .... _____

MY CAN-DO CHANT
"I can ... I will ... I'm good!"

FOOD ITEM	CALS	FATS	CHOLES	CARBS	PROS
Targets	*2000*	*80*	*300*	*250*	*90*
TOTALS					

If you <u>score</u>, you do <u>less</u> & <u>more</u>!

QUOTE OF THE DAY

"Doing nothing is very hard to do ... you never know when you're finished."
Leslie Nielsen

WATER

8	24	40	56	72	88	104	120
0	16	32	48	64	80	96	112	128

BREATHING

AM		Noon		PM	

GOALS

WEIGHT: _____
EXERCISE: _____
SCORE: _____

"If it's to be, it's up to me!"

Personal
Power Performance
Daily Success Scorecard

Week: ___8___   Day: ___2___   Date: _____

Be Your Own Best Boss

Business Matters—*Nothing happens without engagement.*

Primary ~ {40 Points} .... _____
1. Money Makers   _____
2. SAM Actions   _____
Secondary ~ {20 Points}   .... _____
1. R & D   _____
2. Networking   _____
Bizyness ~ {10 Points}   .... _____
1. PATTs   _____
2. G & A   _____

Nutrition—*Controlling our own destiny.*

Calories ~ {7 Points} .... _____
Nutraceuticals ~ {1 Point} .... _____
Hydration ~ {2 Points} .... _____

Exercise—*Do it! Do it right! Do it right now!*

Physical ~ {7 Points}   _____ _____
Breathing ~ {3 Points} .... _____

Reading—*The man who reads is the man who leads.*   {5 Points} .... _____
1. Spirituality ~ {2 Points}   _____
2. Business ~ {2 Points}   _____
3. Recreation ~ {1 Point}   _____

M.B.O.—*My future depends on many things, but mostly on me.*   {3 Points} .... _____
1. Score ~ {1 Point}   _____
2. Plan ~ {1 Point}   _____
3. Save ~ {1 Point}   _____

Relationships—*"SMILE"*   {1 Point} .... _____
Personal Time—*"R & R 4me"*   {1 Point} .... _____

Selling = 4 to 5 hours a day

Total Daily Points ...   *"If not me, who?"*   .... _____
Target for the Day ...   *"If not now, when?*   .... _____

MY CAN-DO CHANT
"I can ... I will ... I'm good!"

FOOD ITEM	CALS	FATS	CHOLES	CARBS	PROS
Targets	*2000*	*80*	*300*	*250*	*90*
TOTALS					

If you <u>score</u>, you do <u>less</u> & <u>more</u>!

QUOTE OF THE DAY

"The secret of getting things done is to act."
Dante Alighieri

WATER

8	24	40	56	72	88	104	120
0	16	32	48	64	80	96	112	128

BREATHING

AM		Noon		PM	

GOALS

WEIGHT: _____
EXERCISE: _____
SCORE: _____

"If it's to be, it's up to me!"

Power Performance
Daily Success Scorecard

Week: _____ 8 _____   Day: _____ 3 _____   Date: _____

Be Your Own Best Boss

Business Matters—*Nothing happens without engagement.*

    Primary ~ {40 Points} .... _____

    1. Money Makers   _____

    2. SAM Actions   _____

    Secondary ~ {20 Points}   .... _____

    1. R & D   _____

    2. Networking   _____

    Bizyness ~ {10 Points}   .... _____

    1. PATTs   _____

    2. G & A   _____

Nutrition—*Controlling our own destiny.*

    Calories ~ {7 Points}.. _____

    Nutraceuticals ~ {1 Point}... _____

    Hydration ~ {2 Points} .... _____

Exercise—*Do it! Do it right! Do it right now!*

    Physical ~ {7 Points}   _____

    Breathing ~ {3 Points} .... _____

Reading—*The man who reads is the man who leads.*   {5 Points} .... _____

    1. Spirituality ~ {2 Points}   _____

    2. Business ~ {2 Points}   _____

    3. Recreation ~ {1 Point}   _____

_M.B.O._—*My future depends on many things, but mostly on me.*   {3 Points} .... _____

    1. Score ~ {1 Point}   _____

    2. Plan ~ {1 Point}   _____

    3. Save ~ {1 Point}   _____

Relationships—*"SMILE"*   {1 Point}......... _____

Personal Time—*"R & R 4me"*   {1 Point}......... _____

Selling = 4 to 5 hours a day

Total Daily Points ...   *"If not me, who?"*   .... _____

Target for the Day ...   *"If not now, when?*   .... _____

My Can-Do Chant
"I can ... I will ... I'm good!"

Food Item	Cals	Fats	Choles	Carbs	Pros
Targets	2000	80	300	250	90
Totals					

If you <u>score</u>, you do <u>less</u> & <u>more</u>!

Quote of the Day

"The fruits of life fall into the hands of those who climb the tree and pick them."
Earl Tupper

Water

8	24	40	56	72	88	104	120
0	16	32	48	64	80	96	112	128

Breathing

AM		Noon		PM	

Goals

Weight: _____
Exercise: _____
Score: _____

"If it's to be, it's up to me!"

Personal
Power Performance
Daily Success Scorecard

Week: _____ 8 _____ Day: _____ 4 _____ Date: _____

Be Your Own Best Boss

Business Matters—*Nothing happens without engagement.*

Primary ~ {40 Points} .... _____

   1. Money Makers   _____

   2. SAM Actions   _____

Secondary ~ {20 Points}   .... _____

   1. R & D   _____

   2. Networking   _____

Bizyness ~ {10 Points}   .... _____

   1. PATTs   _____

   2. G & A   _____

Nutrition—*Controlling our own destiny.*

Calories ~ {7 Points}... _____

Nutraceuticals ~ {1 Point}................................... _____

Hydration ~ {2 Points} .... _____

Exercise—*Do it! Do it right! Do it right now!*

Physical ~ {7 Points}   _____ _____

Breathing ~ {3 Points} .... _____

Reading—*The man who reads is the man who leads.*   {5 Points} .... _____

   1. Spirituality ~ {2 Points}   _____

   2. Business ~ {2 Points}   _____

   3. Recreation ~ {1 Point}   _____

M.B.O.—*My future depends on many things, but mostly on me.*   {3 Points} .... _____

   1. Score ~ {1 Point}   _____

   2. Plan ~ {1 Point}   _____

   3. Save ~ {1 Point}   _____

Relationships—*"SMILE"*   {1 Point} .... _____

Personal Time—*"R & R 4me"*   {1 Point} .... _____

Selling = 4 to 5 hours a day

Total Daily Points ...   *"If not me, who?"*   .... _____

Target for the Day ...   *"If not now, when?*   .... _____

My Can-Do Chant
"I can ... I will ... I'm good!"

Food Item	Cals	Fats	Choles	Carbs	Pros
Targets	*2000*	*80*	*300*	*250*	*90*
Totals					

If you <u>score</u>, you do <u>less</u> & <u>more</u>!

Quote of the Day

"It is not enough to have great qualities; We should also have the management of them."
La Rochefoucauld

Water

8	24	40	56	72	88	104	120
0	16	32	48	64	80	96	112	128

Breathing

AM		Noon		PM	

Goals

Weight: _____
Exercise: _____
Score: _____

"If it's to be, it's up to me!"

Power Performance

Daily Success Scorecard

Week: ___8___   Day: ___5___   Date: _____

Be Your Own Best Boss

Business Matters—*Nothing happens without engagement.*

Primary ~ {40 Points} .... ____

1. Money Makers _____

2. SAM Actions _____

Secondary ~ {20 Points}   .... ____

1. R & D _____

2. Networking _____

Bizyness ~ {10 Points}   .... ____

1. PATTs _____

2. G & A _____

Nutrition—*Controlling our own destiny.*

Calories ~ {7 Points}.. ____

Nutraceuticals ~ {1 Point}................................... ____

Hydration ~ {2 Points} .... ____

Exercise—*Do it! Do it right! Do it right now!*

Physical ~ {7 Points} _____ ____

Breathing ~ {3 Points} .... ____

Reading—*The man who reads is the man who leads.*   {5 Points} .... ____

1. Spirituality ~ {2 Points} _____

2. Business ~ {2 Points} _____

3. Recreation ~ {1 Point} _____

M.B.O.—*My future depends on many things, but mostly on me.*   {3 Points} .... ____

1. Score ~ {1 Point} _____

2. Plan ~ {1 Point} _____

3. Save ~ {1 Point} _____

Relationships—*"SMILE"*   {1 Point} .... ____

Personal Time—*"R & R 4me"*   {1 Point} .... ____

Selling = 4 to 5 hours a day

Total Daily Points ...   *"If not me, who?"*   .... ____

Target for the Day ...   *"If not now, when?*   .... ____

MY CAN-DO CHANT
"I can ... I will ... I'm good!"

FOOD ITEM	CALS	FATS	CHOLES	CARBS	PROS
Targets	*2000*	*80*	*300*	*250*	*90*
TOTALS					

If you <u>score</u>, you do <u>less</u> & <u>more!</u>

QUOTE OF THE DAY

"And in the end, it's not the years in your life that count. It's the life in your years."
Abraham Lincoln

WATER

8	24	40	56	72	88	104	120
0	16	32	48	64	80	96	112	128

BREATHING

AM		Noon		PM	

GOALS

WEIGHT: _____
EXERCISE: _____
SCORE: _____

"If it's to be, it's up to me!"

Personal
Power Performance
Daily Success Scorecard

Week: ___8___   Day: ___6___   Date: _____

Be Your Own Best Boss

Business Matters—*Nothing happens without engagement.*

     Primary ~ {40 Points} .... _____
     1. Money Makers   _____
     2. SAM Actions   _____
     Secondary ~ {20 Points}   .... _____
     1. R & D   _____
     2. Networking   _____
     Bizyness ~ {10 Points}   .... _____
     1. PATTs   _____
     2. G & A   _____

Nutrition—*Controlling our own destiny.*

     Calories ~ {7 Points} .... _____
     Nutraceuticals ~ {1 Point} .... _____
     Hydration ~ {2 Points} .... _____

Exercise—*Do it! Do it right! Do it right now!*

     Physical ~ {7 Points}   _____
     Breathing ~ {3 Points} .... _____

Reading—*The man who reads is the man who leads.*   {5 Points} .... _____
     1. Spirituality ~ {2 Points}   _____
     2. Business ~ {2 Points}   _____
     3. Recreation ~ {1 Point}   _____

M.B.O.—*My future depends on many things, but mostly on me.*   {3 Points} .... _____
     1. Score ~ {1 Point}   _____
     2. Plan ~ {1 Point}   _____
     3. Save ~ {1 Point}   _____

Relationships—*"SMILE"*   {1 Point} .... _____
Personal Time—*"R & R 4me"*   {1 Point} .... _____

Selling = 4 to 5 hours a day

Total Daily Points ...   *"If not me, who?"*   .... _____
Target for the Day ...   *"If not now, when?*   .... _____

MY CAN-DO CHANT
"I can ... I will ... I'm good!"

FOOD ITEM	CALS	FATS	CHOLES	CARBS	PROS
Targets	*2000*	*80*	*300*	*250*	*90*
TOTALS					

If you <u>score</u>, you do <u>less</u> & <u>more!</u>

QUOTE OF THE DAY

"Difficulties mastered are opportunities won."
Winston Churchill

WATER

8	24	40	56	72	88	104	120
0	16	32	48	64	80	96	112	128

BREATHING

AM		Noon		PM	

GOALS

WEIGHT: _____
EXERCISE: _____
SCORE: _____

"If it's to be, it's up to me!"

110

Personal
Power Performance
Daily Success Scorecard

Week: _____8_____   Day: _____7_____   Date: _____

Be Your Own Best Boss

Business Matters—*Nothing happens without engagement.*

   Primary ~ {40 Points} .... _____

   1. Money Makers   _____

   2. SAM Actions   _____

   Secondary ~ {20 Points}   .... _____

   1. R & D   _____

   2. Networking   _____

   Bizyness ~ {10 Points}   .... _____

   1. PATTs   _____

   2. G & A   _____

Nutrition—*Controlling our own destiny.*

   Calories ~ {7 Points} ....

   Nutraceuticals ~ {1 Point} .... _____

   Hydration ~ {2 Points} .... _____

Exercise—*Do it! Do it right! Do it right now!*

   Physical ~ {7 Points}   _____

   Breathing ~ {3 Points} .... _____

Reading—*The man who reads is the man who leads.*   {5 Points} .... _____

   1. Spirituality ~ {2 Points}   _____

   2. Business ~ {2 Points}   _____

   3. Recreation ~ {1 Point}   _____

M.B.O.—*My future depends on many things, but mostly on me.*   {3 Points} .... _____

   1. Score ~ {1 Point}   _____

   2. Plan ~ {1 Point}   _____

   3. Save ~ {1 Point}   _____

Relationships—*"SMILE"*   {1 Point} .... _____

Personal Time—*"R & R 4me"*   {1 Point} .... _____

Selling = 4 to 5 hours a day

Total Daily Points ...   *"If not me, who?"*   .... _____

Target for the Day ...   *"If not now, when?*   .... _____

MY CAN-DO CHANT
"I can ... I will ... I'm good!"

FOOD ITEM	CALS	FATS	CHOLES	CARBS	PROS
Targets	*2000*	*80*	*300*	*250*	*90*
TOTALS					

If you <u>score</u>, you do <u>less</u> & <u>more</u>!

QUOTE OF THE DAY

"Quality is not an act.
It is a habit."
Aristotle

WATER

8	24	40	56	72	88	104	120
0	16	32	48	64	80	96	112	128

BREATHING

AM		Noon		PM	

GOALS

WEIGHT: _____
EXERCISE: _____
SCORE: _____

"If it's to be, it's up to me!"

112

Personal
Power Performance
Daily Success Scorecard

Week: ___9___   Day: ___1___   Date: _____

Be Your Own Best Boss

Business Matters—*Nothing happens without engagement.*

Primary ~ {40 Points} .... _____
1. Money Makers   _____
2. SAM Actions   _____
Secondary ~ {20 Points}   .... _____
1. R & D   _____
2. Networking   _____
Bizyness ~ {10 Points}   .... _____
1. PATTs   _____
2. G & A   _____

Nutrition—*Controlling our own destiny.*

Calories ~ {7 Points}... _____
Nutraceuticals ~ {1 Point}................................... _____
Hydration ~ {2 Points} .... _____

Exercise—*Do it! Do it right! Do it right now!*

Physical ~ {7 Points}   _____ _____
Breathing ~ {3 Points} .... _____

Reading—*The man who reads is the man who leads.*   {5 Points} .... _____
1. Spirituality ~ {2 Points}   _____
2. Business ~ {2 Points}   _____
3. Recreation ~ {1 Point}   _____

M.B.O.—*My future depends on many things, but mostly on me.*   {3 Points} ....
1. Score ~ {1 Point}   _____
2. Plan ~ {1 Point}   _____
3. Save ~ {1 Point}   _____

Relationships—*"SMILE"*   {1 Point} ....

Personal Time—*"R & R 4me"*   {1 Point} .... _____

Selling = 4 to 5 hours a day

Total Daily Points ...   *"If not me, who?"*   .... _____

Target for the Day ...   *"If not now, when?*   .... _____

My Can-Do Chant
"I can … I will … I'm good!"

Food Item	Cals	Fats	Choles	Carbs	Pros
Targets	*2000*	*80*	*300*	*250*	*90*
Totals					

If you <u>score</u>, you do <u>less</u> & <u>more</u>!

Quote of the Day

"Unless a man undertakes more than he possibly can do, he will never do all that he can."
Henry Drummond

Water

8	24	40	56	72	88	104	120
0	16	32	48	64	80	96	112	128

Breathing

AM		Noon		PM	

Goals

WEIGHT: _____
EXERCISE: _____
SCORE: _____

"If it's to be, it's up to me!"

114

Power Performance

Daily Success Scorecard

Week: ___9___   Day: ___2___   Date: _____

Be Your Own Best Boss

Business Matters—*Nothing happens without engagement.*

    Primary ~ {40 Points} .... _____

    1. Money Makers   _____

    2. SAM Actions   _____

    Secondary ~ {20 Points}   .... _____

    1. R & D   _____

    2. Networking   _____

    Bizyness ~ {10 Points}   .... _____

    1. PATTs   _____

    2. G & A   _____

Nutrition—*Controlling our own destiny.*

    Calories ~ {7 Points}.. _____

    Nutraceuticals ~ {1 Point}.. _____

    Hydration ~ {2 Points} .... _____

Exercise—*Do it! Do it right! Do it right now!*

    Physical ~ {7 Points}   _____ _____

    Breathing ~ {3 Points} .... _____

Reading—*The man who reads is the man who leads.*   {5 Points} .... _____

    1. Spirituality ~ {2 Points}   _____

    2. Business ~ {2 Points}   _____

    3. Recreation ~ {1 Point}   _____

M.B.O.—*My future depends on many things, but mostly on me.* {3 Points} .... _____

    1. Score ~ {1 Point}   _____

    2. Plan ~ {1 Point}   _____

    3. Save ~ {1 Point}   _____

Relationships—*"SMILE"*   {1 Point}......... _____

Personal Time—*"R & R 4me"*   {1 Point}......... _____

Selling = 4 to 5 hours a day

Total Daily Points ...   *"If not me, who?"* .... _____

Target for the Day ...   *"If not now, when?* .... _____

MY CAN-DO CHANT
"I can ... I will ... I'm good!"

FOOD ITEM	CALS	FATS	CHOLES	CARBS	PROS
Targets	*2000*	*80*	*300*	*250*	*90*
TOTALS					

If you <u>score</u>, you do <u>less</u> & <u>more!</u>

QUOTE OF THE DAY

"If you do not know where you are going, every road will get you nowhere."
Henry Kissinger

WATER

8	24	40	56	72	88	104	120
0	16	32	48	64	80	96	112	128

BREATHING

AM		Noon		PM	

GOALS

WEIGHT: _____
EXERCISE: _____
SCORE: _____

"If it's to be, it's up to me!"

Power Performance

Daily Success Scorecard

Week: ___9___   Day: ___3___   Date: _____

Be Your Own Best Boss

Business Matters—*Nothing happens without engagement.*

    Primary ~ {40 Points} .... _____
    1. Money Makers   _____
    2. SAM Actions   _____
    Secondary ~ {20 Points}   .... _____
    1. R & D   _____
    2. Networking   _____
    Bizyness ~ {10 Points}   .... _____
    1. PATTs   _____
    2. G & A   _____

Nutrition—*Controlling our own destiny.*

    Calories ~ {7 Points} .... _____
    Nutraceuticals ~ {1 Point} .... _____
    Hydration ~ {2 Points} .... _____

Exercise—*Do it! Do it right! Do it right now!*

    Physical ~ {7 Points}   _____ _____
    Breathing ~ {3 Points} .... _____

Reading—*The man who reads is the man who leads.*   {5 Points} .... _____

    1. Spirituality ~ {2 Points}   _____
    2. Business ~ {2 Points}   _____
    3. Recreation ~ {1 Point}   _____

M.B.O.—*My future depends on many things, but mostly on me.*   {3 Points} .... _____

    1. Score ~ {1 Point}   _____
    2. Plan ~ {1 Point}   _____
    3. Save ~ {1 Point}   _____

Relationships—*"SMILE"*   {1 Point} .... _____

Personal Time—*"R & R 4me"*   {1 Point} .... _____

Selling = 4 to 5 hours a day

Total Daily Points ...   *"If not me, who?"*   .... _____

Target for the Day ...   *"If not now, when?*   .... _____

My Can-Do Chant
"I can ... I will ... I'm good!"

FOOD ITEM	CALS	FATS	CHOLES	CARBS	PROS
Targets	*2000*	*80*	*300*	*250*	*90*
TOTALS					

If you <u>score</u>, you do <u>less</u> & <u>more</u>!

QUOTE OF THE DAY

"Performance is your actions. The result is your reality."
R. Wayne Kukowski

WATER

8	24	40	56	72	88	104	120
0	16	32	48	64	80	96	112	128

BREATHING

AM		Noon		PM	

GOALS

WEIGHT: _____
EXERCISE: _____
SCORE: _____

"If it's to be, it's up to me!"

118

Personal
Power Performance
Daily Success Scorecard

Week: ____9____   Day: ____4____   Date: _____

Be Your Own Best Boss

__Business Matters__—*Nothing happens without engagement.*

    Primary ~ {40 Points} .... _____

    1. Money Makers   _____

    2. SAM Actions   _____

    Secondary ~ {20 Points}   .... _____

    1. R & D   _____

    2. Networking   _____

    Bizyness ~ {10 Points}   .... _____

    1. PATTs   _____

    2. G & A   _____

__Nutrition__—*Controlling our own destiny.*

    Calories ~ {7 Points}... _____

    Nutraceuticals ~ {1 Point}................................... _____

    Hydration ~ {2 Points} .... _____

__Exercise__—*Do it! Do it right! Do it right now!*

    Physical ~ {7 Points}   _____ _____

    Breathing ~ {3 Points} .... _____

__Reading__—*The man who reads is the man who leads.*   {5 Points} .... _____

    1. Spirituality ~ {2 Points}   _____

    2. Business ~ {2 Points}   _____

    3. Recreation ~ {1 Point}   _____

__M.B.O.__—*My future depends on many things, but mostly on me.*   {3 Points} .... _____

    1. Score ~ {1 Point}   _____

    2. Plan ~ {1 Point}   _____

    3. Save ~ {1 Point}   _____

__Relationships__—*"SMILE"*   {1 Point} .... _____

__Personal Time__—*"R & R 4me"*   {1 Point} .... _____

Selling = 4 to 5 hours a day

Total Daily Points ...   *"If not me, who?"*   .... _____

Target for the Day ...   *"If not now, when?*   .... _____

My Can-Do Chant
"I can ... I will ... I'm good!"

Food Item	Cals	Fats	Choles	Carbs	Pros
Targets	*2000*	*80*	*300*	*250*	*90*
Totals					

If you <u>score</u>, you do <u>less</u> & <u>more</u>!

Quote of the Day

"Procrastination is the thief of time."
Edward Young

Water

8	24	40	56	72	88	104	120
0	16	32	48	64	80	96	112	128

Breathing

AM		Noon		PM	

Goals

Weight:	_____
Exercise:	_____
Score:	_____

"If it's to be, it's up to me!"

Power Performance

Daily Success Scorecard

Week: _____9_____   Day: _____5_____   Date: _____

Be Your Own Best Boss

Business Matters—*Nothing happens without engagement.*

Primary ~ {40 Points} .... _____
1. Money Makers   _____
2. SAM Actions   _____
Secondary ~ {20 Points}   .... _____
1. R & D   _____
2. Networking   _____
Bizyness ~ {10 Points}   .... _____
1. PATTs   _____
2. G & A   _____

Nutrition—*Controlling our own destiny.*

Calories ~ {7 Points}... _____
Nutraceuticals ~ {1 Point}... _____
Hydration ~ {2 Points} .... _____

Exercise—*Do it! Do it right! Do it right now!*

Physical ~ {7 Points}   _____ _____
Breathing ~ {3 Points} .... _____

Reading—*The man who reads is the man who leads.*   {5 Points} .... _____
1. Spirituality ~ {2 Points}   _____
2. Business ~ {2 Points}   _____
3. Recreation ~ {1 Point}   _____

M.B.O.—*My future depends on many things, but mostly on me.*   {3 Points} .... _____
1. Score ~ {1 Point}   _____
2. Plan ~ {1 Point}   _____
3. Save ~ {1 Point}   _____

Relationships—*"SMILE"*   {1 Point}......... _____
Personal Time—*"R & R 4me"*   {1 Point}......... _____

Selling = 4 to 5 hours a day

Total Daily Points ...   *"If not me, who?"*   .... _____
Target for the Day ...   *"If not now, when?*   .... _____

My Can-Do Chant
"I can … I will … I'm good!"

Food Item	Cals	Fats	Choles	Carbs	Pros
Targets	*2000*	*80*	*300*	*250*	*90*
Totals					

If you <u>score</u>, you do <u>less</u> & <u>more!</u>

Quote of the Day

"You are younger today than you will ever be again. Make use of it for the sake of tomorrow."
Norman Cousins

Water

8	24	40	56	72	88	104	120
0	16	32	48	64	80	96	112	128

Breathing

AM		Noon		PM	

Goals

Weight:	_____
Exercise:	_____
Score:	_____

"If it's to be, it's up to me!"

Personal
Power Performance
Daily Success Scorecard

Week: _____ 9 _____ Day: _____ 6 _____ Date: _____

Be Your Own Best Boss

Business Matters—*Nothing happens without engagement.*

    Primary ~ {40 Points} .... _____
    1. Money Makers   _____
    2. SAM Actions   _____
    Secondary ~ {20 Points}   .... _____
    1. R & D   _____
    2. Networking   _____
    Bizyness ~ {10 Points}   .... _____
    1. PATTs   _____
    2. G & A   _____

Nutrition—*Controlling our own destiny.*

    Calories ~ {7 Points}.. _____
    Nutraceuticals ~ {1 Point}... _____
    Hydration ~ {2 Points} .... _____

Exercise—*Do it! Do it right! Do it right now!*

    Physical ~ {7 Points}   _____ _____
    Breathing ~ {3 Points} .... _____

Reading—*The man who reads is the man who leads.*   {5 Points} .... _____

    1. Spirituality ~ {2 Points}   _____
    2. Business ~ {2 Points}   _____
    3. Recreation ~ {1 Point}   _____

M.B.O.—*My future depends on many things, but mostly on me.*   {3 Points} .... _____

    1. Score ~ {1 Point}   _____
    2. Plan ~ {1 Point}   _____
    3. Save ~ {1 Point}   _____

Relationships—*"SMILE"*   {1 Point} .... _____

Personal Time—*"R & R 4me"*   {1 Point} .... _____

Selling = 4 to 5 hours a day

Total Daily Points ...   *"If not me, who?"*   .... _____
Target for the Day ...   *"If not now, when?*   .... _____

My Can-Do Chant
"I can ... I will ... I'm good!"

Food Item	Cals	Fats	Choles	Carbs	Pros
Targets	*2000*	*80*	*300*	*250*	*90*
TOTALS					

If you <u>score</u>, you do <u>less</u> & <u>more</u>!

QUOTE OF THE DAY

"Start your day the night before, get enough sleep."
Peter Biadasz

WATER

8	24	40	56	72	88	104	120
0	16	32	48	64	80	96	112	128

BREATHING

AM		Noon		PM	

GOALS

WEIGHT: _____
EXERCISE: _____
SCORE: _____

"If it's to be, it's up to me!"

Power Performance
Daily Success Scorecard

Week: _____9_____ Day: _____7_____ Date: _____

Be Your Own Best Boss

Business Matters—*Nothing happens without engagement.*

    Primary ~ {40 Points} .... _____

    1. Money Makers _____

    2. SAM Actions _____

    Secondary ~ {20 Points} .... _____

    1. R & D _____

    2. Networking _____

    Bizyness ~ {10 Points} .... _____

    1. PATTs _____

    2. G & A _____

Nutrition—*Controlling our own destiny.*

    Calories ~ {7 Points}.. _____

    Nutraceuticals ~ {1 Point}.. _____

    Hydration ~ {2 Points} .... _____

Exercise—*Do it! Do it right! Do it right now!*

    Physical ~ {7 Points} _____

    Breathing ~ {3 Points} .... _____

Reading—*The man who reads is the man who leads.*   {5 Points} .... _____

    1. Spirituality ~ {2 Points} _____

    2. Business ~ {2 Points} _____

    3. Recreation ~ {1 Point} _____

M.B.O.—*My future depends on many things, but mostly on me.*   {3 Points} .... _____

    1. Score ~ {1 Point} _____

    2. Plan ~ {1 Point} _____

    3. Save ~ {1 Point} _____

Relationships—*"SMILE"*   {1 Point}......... _____

Personal Time—*"R & R 4me"*   {1 Point}......... _____

Selling = 4 to 5 hours a day

Total Daily Points ...   *"If not me, who?"*   .... _____

Target for the Day ...   *"If not now, when?*   .... _____

MY CAN-DO CHANT
"I can ... I will ... I'm good!"

FOOD ITEM	CALS	FATS	CHOLES	CARBS	PROS
Targets	*2000*	*80*	*300*	*250*	*90*
TOTALS					

If you <u>score</u>, you do <u>less</u> & <u>more</u>!

QUOTE OF THE DAY

"Life is like riding a bicycle. You don't fall off unless you plan to stop peddling."
Claude Pepper

WATER

8	24	40	56	72	88	104	120
0	16	32	48	64	80	96	112	128

BREATHING

AM		Noon		PM	

GOALS

WEIGHT: _____
EXERCISE: _____
SCORE: _____

"If it's to be, it's up to me!"

Power Performance
Daily Success Scorecard

Week: _____10_____   Day: _____1_____   Date: _____

Be Your Own Best Boss

Business Matters—*Nothing happens without engagement.*

    Primary ~ {40 Points} .... _____

    1. Money Makers   _____

    2. SAM Actions   _____

    Secondary ~ {20 Points}   .... _____

    1. R & D   _____

    2. Networking   _____

    Bizyness ~ {10 Points}   .... _____

    1. PATTs   _____

    2. G & A   _____

Nutrition—*Controlling our own destiny.*

    Calories ~ {7 Points} .... _____

    Nutraceuticals ~ {1 Point} .... _____

    Hydration ~ {2 Points} .... _____

Exercise—*Do it! Do it right! Do it right now!*

    Physical ~ {7 Points}   _____ _____

    Breathing ~ {3 Points} .... _____

Reading—*The man who reads is the man who leads.*   {5 Points} .... _____

    1. Spirituality ~ {2 Points}   _____

    2. Business ~ {2 Points}   _____

    3. Recreation ~ {1 Point}   _____

M.B.O.—*My future depends on many things, but mostly on me.*   {3 Points} .... _____

    1. Score ~ {1 Point}   _____

    2. Plan ~ {1 Point}   _____

    3. Save ~ {1 Point}   _____

Relationships—*"SMILE"*   {1 Point} .... _____

Personal Time—*"R & R 4me"*   {1 Point} .... _____

Selling = 4 to 5 hours a day

Total Daily Points ...   *"If not me, who?"*   .... _____

Target for the Day ...   *"If not now, when?*   .... _____

My Can-Do Chant
"I can … I will … I'm good!"

Food Item	Cals	Fats	Choles	Carbs	Pros
Targets	*2000*	*80*	*300*	*250*	*90*
Totals					

If you <u>score</u>, you do <u>less</u> & <u>more</u>!

Quote of the Day

"Even if you're on the right track, you'll get run over if you just sit there."
Will Rogers

Water

8	24	40	56	72	88	104	120
0	16	32	48	64	80	96	112	128

Breathing

AM		Noon		PM	

Goals

Weight:	_____
Exercise:	_____
Score:	_____

"If it's to be, it's up to me!"

Power Performance
Daily Success Scorecard

Week: 10   Day: 2   Date: _____

Be Your Own Best Boss

Business Matters—*Nothing happens without engagement.*

    Primary ~ {40 Points} .... _____

    1. Money Makers   _____

    2. SAM Actions   _____

    Secondary ~ {20 Points}   .... _____

    1. R & D   _____

    2. Networking   _____

    Bizyness ~ {10 Points}   .... _____

    1. PATTs   _____

    2. G & A   _____

Nutrition—*Controlling our own destiny.*

    Calories ~ {7 Points}...

    Nutraceuticals ~ {1 Point}...................................... _____

    Hydration ~ {2 Points} .... _____

Exercise—*Do it! Do it right! Do it right now!*

    Physical ~ {7 Points}   _____ _____

    Breathing ~ {3 Points} ....

Reading—*The man who reads is the man who leads.*   {5 Points} .... _____

    1. Spirituality ~ {2 Points}   _____

    2. Business ~ {2 Points}   _____

    3. Recreation ~ {1 Point}   _____

M.B.O.—*My future depends on many things, but mostly on me.*   {3 Points} ....

    1. Score ~ {1 Point}   _____

    2. Plan ~ {1 Point}   _____

    3. Save ~ {1 Point}   _____

Relationships—*"SMILE"*   {1 Point} .... _____

Personal Time—*"R & R 4me"*   {1 Point} .... _____

Selling = 4 to 5 hours a day

Total Daily Points ...   *"If not me, who?"*   .... _____

Target for the Day ...   *"If not now, when?*   .... _____

MY CAN-DO CHANT
"I can … I will … I'm good!"

FOOD ITEM	CALS	FATS	CHOLES	CARBS	PROS
Targets	*2000*	*80*	*300*	*250*	*90*
TOTALS					

If you <u>score</u>, you do <u>less</u> & <u>more</u>!

QUOTE OF THE DAY

"Concern yourself not with what you tried and failed in, but what is still possible for you to do."
Pope John XXIII

WATER

8	24	40	56	72	88	104	120
0 16	32	48	64	80	96	112	128

BREATHING

AM		Noon		PM	

GOALS

WEIGHT: _____
EXERCISE: _____
SCORE: _____

"If it's to be, it's up to me!"

130

Power Performance

Daily Success Scorecard

Week: _____10_____   Day: _____3_____   Date: _____

Be Your Own Best Boss

Business Matters—*Nothing happens without engagement.*

     Primary ~ {40 Points} .... _____

     1. Money Makers   _____

     2. SAM Actions   _____

     Secondary ~ {20 Points}   .... _____

     1. R & D   _____

     2. Networking   _____

     Bizyness ~ {10 Points}   .... _____

     1. PATTs   _____

     2. G & A   _____

Nutrition—*Controlling our own destiny.*

     Calories ~ {7 Points}.. _____

     Nutraceuticals ~ {1 Point}... _____

     Hydration ~ {2 Points} .... _____

Exercise—*Do it! Do it right! Do it right now!*

     Physical ~ {7 Points}   _____ _____

     Breathing ~ {3 Points} .... _____

Reading—*The man who reads is the man who leads.*   {5 Points} .... _____

     1. Spirituality ~ {2 Points}   _____

     2. Business ~ {2 Points}   _____

     3. Recreation ~ {1 Point}   _____

M.B.O.—*My future depends on many things, but mostly on me.*   {3 Points} .... _____

     1. Score ~ {1 Point}   _____

     2. Plan ~ {1 Point}   _____

     3. Save ~ {1 Point}   _____

Relationships—*"SMILE"*   {1 Point}......... _____

Personal Time—*"R & R 4me"*   {1 Point}......... _____

Selling = 4 to 5 hours a day

Total Daily Points ...   *"If not me, who?"*   .... _____

Target for the Day ...   *"If not now, when?*   .... _____

MY CAN-DO CHANT
"I can ... I will ... I'm good!"

FOOD ITEM	CALS	FATS	CHOLES	CARBS	PROS
Targets	*2000*	*80*	*300*	*250*	*90*
TOTALS					

If you <u>score</u>, you do <u>less</u> & <u>more</u>!

QUOTE OF THE DAY

"Ability is what you're capable of doing. Motivation determines what you do. Attitude determines how well you do it."
Raymond Chandler

WATER

8	24	40	56	72	88	104	120
0 16	32	48	64	80	96	112	128

BREATHING

AM		Noon		PM	

GOALS

WEIGHT:	_____
EXERCISE:	_____
SCORE:	_____

"If it's to be, it's up to me!"

Personal
Power Performance
Daily Success Scorecard

Week: _____10_____   Day: _____4_____   Date: _____

Be Your Own Best Boss

Business Matters—*Nothing happens without engagement.*

Primary ~ {40 Points} .... _____
1. Money Makers   _____
2. SAM Actions   _____
Secondary ~ {20 Points}   .... _____
1. R & D   _____
2. Networking   _____
Bizyness ~ {10 Points}   .... _____
1. PATTs   _____
2. G & A   _____

Nutrition—*Controlling our own destiny.*

Calories ~ {7 Points} .... _____
Nutraceuticals ~ {1 Point} .... _____
Hydration ~ {2 Points} .... _____

Exercise—*Do it! Do it right! Do it right now!*

Physical ~ {7 Points}   _____ _____
Breathing ~ {3 Points} .... _____

Reading—*The man who reads is the man who leads.*   {5 Points} .... _____
1. Spirituality ~ {2 Points}   _____
2. Business ~ {2 Points}   _____
3. Recreation ~ {1 Point}   _____

M.B.O.—*My future depends on many things, but mostly on me.*   {3 Points} ....
1. Score ~ {1 Point}   _____
2. Plan ~ {1 Point}   _____
3. Save ~ {1 Point}   _____

Relationships—*"SMILE"*   {1 Point} .... _____
Personal Time—*"R & R 4me"*   {1 Point} .... _____

Selling = 4 to 5 hours a day

Total Daily Points ...   *"If not me, who?"*   .... _____
Target for the Day ...   *"If not now, when?*   .... _____

My Can-Do Chant
"I can ... I will ... I'm good!"

Food Item	Cals	Fats	Choles	Carbs	Pros
Targets	*2000*	*80*	*300*	*250*	*90*
Totals					

If you <u>score</u>, you do <u>less</u> & <u>more!</u>

Quote of the Day
"It has long since come to my attention that people of accomplishment rarely sit back and let things happen to them. They went out and happened to things."
Elinor Smith

Water

8	24	40	56	72	88	104	120
0	16	32	48	64	80	96	112	128

Breathing

AM		Noon		PM	

Goals

Weight:	_____
Exercise:	_____
Score:	_____

"If it's to be, it's up to me!"

Power Performance

Daily Success Scorecard

Week: ___10___   Day: ___5___   Date: _____

Be Your Own Best Boss

Business Matters—*Nothing happens without engagement.*

Primary ~ {40 Points} .... _____

  1. Money Makers   _____

  2. SAM Actions   _____

Secondary ~ {20 Points}   .... _____

  1. R & D   _____

  2. Networking   _____

Bizyness ~ {10 Points}   .... _____

  1. PATTs   _____

  2. G & A   _____

Nutrition—*Controlling our own destiny.*

Calories ~ {7 Points}... _____

Nutraceuticals ~ {1 Point}.................................... _____

Hydration ~ {2 Points} .... _____

Exercise—*Do it! Do it right! Do it right now!*

Physical ~ {7 Points}   _____ _____

Breathing ~ {3 Points} .... _____

Reading—*The man who reads is the man who leads.*   {5 Points} .... _____

  1. Spirituality ~ {2 Points}   _____

  2. Business ~ {2 Points}   _____

  3. Recreation ~ {1 Point}   _____

M.B.O.—*My future depends on many things, but mostly on me.*   {3 Points} .... _____

  1. Score ~ {1 Point}   _____

  2. Plan ~ {1 Point}   _____

  3. Save ~ {1 Point}   _____

Relationships—*"SMILE"*   {1 Point} .... _____

Personal Time—*"R & R 4me"*   {1 Point} .... _____

Selling = 4 to 5 hours a day

Total Daily Points ...   *"If not me, who?"*   .... _____

Target for the Day ...   *"If not now, when?*   .... _____

MY CAN-DO CHANT
"I can ... I will ... I'm good!"

FOOD ITEM	CALS	FATS	CHOLES	CARBS	PROS
Targets	*2000*	*80*	*300*	*250*	*90*
TOTALS					

If you <u>score</u>, you do <u>less</u> & <u>more</u>!

QUOTE OF THE DAY
"The people who get on in this world are the people who get up and look for the circumstances they want, and, if they can't find them, make them."
George Bernard Shaw

WATER

8	24	40	56	72	88	104	120
0	16	32	48	64	80	96	112	128

BREATHING

AM		Noon		PM	

GOALS

WEIGHT: _____
EXERCISE: _____
SCORE: _____

"If it's to be, it's up to me!"

Power Performance

Daily Success Scorecard

Week: ___10___ Day: ___6___ Date: _____

Be Your Own Best Boss

Business Matters—*Nothing happens without engagement.*

Primary ~ {40 Points} .... _____
1. Money Makers _____
2. SAM Actions _____
Secondary ~ {20 Points} .... _____
1. R & D _____
2. Networking _____
Bizyness ~ {10 Points} .... _____
1. PATTs _____
2. G & A _____

Nutrition—*Controlling our own destiny.*

Calories ~ {7 Points} .... _____
Nutraceuticals ~ {1 Point} .... _____
Hydration ~ {2 Points} .... _____

Exercise—*Do it! Do it right! Do it right now!*

Physical ~ {7 Points} _____ _____
Breathing ~ {3 Points} .... _____

Reading—*The man who reads is the man who leads.* {5 Points} .... _____
1. Spirituality ~ {2 Points} _____
2. Business ~ {2 Points} _____
3. Recreation ~ {1 Point} _____

M.B.O.—*My future depends on many things, but mostly on me.* {3 Points} .... _____
1. Score ~ {1 Point} _____
2. Plan ~ {1 Point} _____
3. Save ~ {1 Point} _____

Relationships—*"SMILE"* {1 Point} .... _____

Personal Time—*"R & R 4me"* {1 Point} .... _____

Selling = 4 to 5 hours a day

Total Daily Points ... *"If not me, who?"* .... _____
Target for the Day ... *"If not now, when?* .... _____

MY CAN-DO CHANT
"I can ... I will ... I'm good!"

FOOD ITEM	CALS	FATS	CHOLES	CARBS	PROS
Targets	*2000*	*80*	*300*	*250*	*90*
TOTALS					

If you <u>score</u>, you do <u>less</u> & <u>more</u>!

QUOTE OF THE DAY

"Nothing will ever be attempted if all possible objections must be first overcome."

Samuel Johnson

WATER

8	24	40	56	72	88	104	120
0	16	32	48	64	80	96	112	128

BREATHING

AM		Noon		PM	

GOALS

WEIGHT: _____

EXERCISE: _____

SCORE: _____

"If it's to be, it's up to me!"

Power Performance

Daily Success Scorecard

Week: __10__   Day: __7__   Date: _____

Be Your Own Best Boss

Business Matters—*Nothing happens without engagement.*

    Primary ~ {40 Points} .... _____

    1. Money Makers   _____

    2. SAM Actions   _____

    Secondary ~ {20 Points}   .... _____

    1. R & D   _____

    2. Networking   _____

    Bizyness ~ {10 Points}   .... _____

    1. PATTs   _____

    2. G & A   _____

Nutrition—*Controlling our own destiny.*

    Calories ~ {7 Points}.. _____

    Nutraceuticals ~ {1 Point}.. _____

    Hydration ~ {2 Points} .... _____

Exercise—*Do it! Do it right! Do it right now!*

    Physical ~ {7 Points}   _____ _____

    Breathing ~ {3 Points} .... _____

Reading—*The man who reads is the man who leads.*   {5 Points} .... _____

    1. Spirituality ~ {2 Points}   _____

    2. Business ~ {2 Points}   _____

    3. Recreation ~ {1 Point}   _____

M.B.O.—*My future depends on many things, but mostly on me.*   {3 Points} .... _____

    1. Score ~ {1 Point}   _____

    2. Plan ~ {1 Point}   _____

    3. Save ~ {1 Point}   _____

Relationships—*"SMILE"*   {1 Point}......... _____

Personal Time—*"R & R 4me"*   {1 Point}......... _____

Selling = 4 to 5 hours a day

Total Daily Points ...   *"If not me, who?"*   .... _____

Target for the Day ...   *"If not now, when?*   .... _____

My Can-Do Chant
"I can … I will … I'm good!"

Food Item	Cals	Fats	Choles	Carbs	Pros
Targets	*2000*	*80*	*300*	*250*	*90*
Totals					

If you <u>score</u>, you do <u>less</u> & <u>more</u>!

Quote of the Day

"Knowing is not enough; we must apply.
Willing is not enough; we must do."
Johann Goethe

Water

8	24	40	56	72	88	104	120
0	16	32	48	64	80	96	112	128

Breathing

AM		Noon		PM	

Goals

Weight: _____
Exercise: _____
Score: _____

"If it's to be, it's up to me!"

Power Performance

Daily Success Scorecard

Week: _____11_____   Day: _____1_____   Date: _____

Be Your Own Best Boss

Business Matters—*Nothing happens without engagement.*

Primary ~ {40 Points} .... _____
1. Money Makers   _____
2. SAM Actions   _____
Secondary ~ {20 Points}   .... _____
1. R & D   _____
2. Networking   _____
Bizyness ~ {10 Points}   .... _____
1. PATTs   _____
2. G & A   _____

Nutrition—*Controlling our own destiny.*

Calories ~ {7 Points}.. _____
Nutraceuticals ~ {1 Point}...................................... _____
Hydration ~ {2 Points} .... _____

Exercise—*Do it! Do it right! Do it right now!*

Physical ~ {7 Points}   _____ _____
Breathing ~ {3 Points} .... _____

Reading—*The man who reads is the man who leads.*   {5 Points} .... _____
1. Spirituality ~ {2 Points}   _____
2. Business ~ {2 Points}   _____
3. Recreation ~ {1 Point}   _____

M.B.O.—*My future depends on many things, but mostly on me.*   {3 Points} .... _____
1. Score ~ {1 Point}   _____
2. Plan ~ {1 Point}   _____
3. Save ~ {1 Point}   _____

Relationships—*"SMILE"*   {1 Point}......... _____
Personal Time—*"R & R 4me"*   {1 Point}......... _____

Selling = 4 to 5 hours a day

Total Daily Points ...   *"If not me, who?"*   .... _____
Target for the Day ...   *"If not now, when?*   .... _____

My Can-Do Chant
"I can … I will … I'm good!"

Food Item	Cals	Fats	Choles	Carbs	Pros
Targets	*2000*	*80*	*300*	*250*	*90*
Totals					

If you <u>score</u>, you do <u>less</u> & <u>more</u>!

Quote of the Day

"Efforts and courage are not enough without purpose and direction."
John F. Kennedy

Water

8	24	40	56	72	88	104	120
0	16	32	48	64	80	96	112	128

Breathing

AM		Noon		PM	

Goals

Weight:	
Exercise:	
Score:	

"If it's to be, it's up to me!"

Power Performance

Daily Success Scorecard

Week: ___11___   Day: ___2___   Date: _____

Be Your Own Best Boss

Business Matters—*Nothing happens without engagement.*

Primary ~ {40 Points} .... _____
1. Money Makers   _____
2. SAM Actions   _____
Secondary ~ {20 Points}   .... _____
1. R & D   _____
2. Networking   _____
Bizyness ~ {10 Points}   .... _____
1. PATTs   _____
2. G & A   _____

Nutrition—*Controlling our own destiny.*

Calories ~ {7 Points}... _____
Nutraceuticals ~ {1 Point}... _____
Hydration ~ {2 Points} .... _____

Exercise—*Do it! Do it right! Do it right now!*

Physical ~ {7 Points}   _____ _____
Breathing ~ {3 Points} .... _____

Reading—*The man who reads is the man who leads.*   {5 Points} .... _____
1. Spirituality ~ {2 Points}   _____
2. Business ~ {2 Points}   _____
3. Recreation ~ {1 Point}   _____

M.B.O.—*My future depends on many things, but mostly on me.*   {3 Points} .... _____
1. Score ~ {1 Point}   _____
2. Plan ~ {1 Point}   _____
3. Save ~ {1 Point}   _____

Relationships—*"SMILE"*   {1 Point}......... _____
Personal Time—*"R & R 4me"*   {1 Point}......... _____

Selling = 4 to 5 hours a day

Total Daily Points ...   *"If not me, who?"*   .... **_____**
Target for the Day ...   *"If not now, when?"* .... **_____**

My Can-Do Chant
"I can ... I will ... I'm good!"

Food Item	Cals	Fats	Choles	Carbs	Pros
Targets	*2000*	*80*	*300*	*250*	*90*
Totals					

If you <u>score</u>, you do <u>less</u> & <u>more</u>!

Quote of the Day

"There are two ways of exerting one's strength: one is pushing down, the other is pulling up."
Booker T. Washington

Water

8	24	40	56	72	88	104	120
0	16	32	48	64	80	96	112	128

Breathing

AM		Noon		PM	

Goals

Weight: _____
Exercise: _____
Score: _____

"If it's to be, it's up to me!"

144

Power Performance
Daily Success Scorecard

Week: _____11_____ Day: _____3_____ Date: _____

Be Your Own Best Boss

Business Matters—*Nothing happens without engagement.*

Primary ~ {40 Points} .... _____
1. Money Makers _____
2. SAM Actions _____
Secondary ~ {20 Points} .... _____
1. R & D _____
2. Networking _____
Bizyness ~ {10 Points} .... _____
1. PATTs _____
2. G & A _____

Nutrition—*Controlling our own destiny.*

Calories ~ {7 Points}.. _____
Nutraceuticals ~ {1 Point}................................ _____
Hydration ~ {2 Points} .... _____

Exercise—*Do it! Do it right! Do it right now!*

Physical ~ {7 Points} _____ _____
Breathing ~ {3 Points} .... _____

Reading—*The man who reads is the man who leads.* {5 Points} .... _____
1. Spirituality ~ {2 Points} _____
2. Business ~ {2 Points} _____
3. Recreation ~ {1 Point} _____

M.B.O.—*My future depends on many things, but mostly on me.* {3 Points} .... _____
1. Score ~ {1 Point} _____
2. Plan ~ {1 Point} _____
3. Save ~ {1 Point} _____

Relationships—*"SMILE"* {1 Point} .... _____
Personal Time—*"R & R 4me"* {1 Point} .... _____

Selling = 4 to 5 hours a day

Total Daily Points ... *"If not me, who?"* .... _____
Target for the Day ... *"If not now, when?"* .... _____

My Can-Do Chant
"I can … I will … I'm good!"

Food Item	Cals	Fats	Choles	Carbs	Pros
Targets	*2000*	*80*	*300*	*250*	*90*
Totals					

If you <u>score</u>, you do <u>less</u> & <u>more</u>!

Quote of the Day

"Hard work spotlights the character of people: some turn up their sleeves, some turn up their noses and some don't turn up at all."
Sam Ewing

Water

8	24	40	56	72	88	104	120
0	16	32	48	64	80	96	112	128

Breathing

AM		Noon		PM	

Goals

Weight: _____
Exercise: _____
Score: _____

"If it's to be, it's up to me!"

Power Performance
Daily Success Scorecard

Week: 11   Day: 4   Date: _____

Be Your Own Best Boss

Business Matters—*Nothing happens without engagement.*

    Primary ~ {40 Points} .... _____

    1. Money Makers   _____

    2. SAM Actions   _____

    Secondary ~ {20 Points}   .... _____

    1. R & D   _____

    2. Networking   _____

    Bizyness ~ {10 Points}   .... _____

    1. PATTs   _____

    2. G & A   _____

Nutrition—*Controlling our own destiny.*

    Calories ~ {7 Points}.. _____

    Nutraceuticals ~ {1 Point}...................................... _____

    Hydration ~ {2 Points} .... _____

Exercise—*Do it! Do it right! Do it right now!*

    Physical ~ {7 Points}   _____ _____

    Breathing ~ {3 Points} .... _____

Reading—*The man who reads is the man who leads.*   {5 Points} .... _____

    1. Spirituality ~ {2 Points}   _____

    2. Business ~ {2 Points}   _____

    3. Recreation ~ {1 Point}   _____

M.B.O.—*My future depends on many things, but mostly on me.*   {3 Points} .... _____

    1. Score ~ {1 Point}   _____

    2. Plan ~ {1 Point}   _____

    3. Save ~ {1 Point}   _____

Relationships—*"SMILE"*   {1 Point}......... _____

Personal Time—*"R & R 4me"*   {1 Point}......... _____

Selling = 4 to 5 hours a day

Total Daily Points ...   *"If not me, who?"*   .... _____

Target for the Day ...   *"If not now, when?"*   .... _____

My Can-Do Chant
"I can ... I will ... I'm good!"

Food Item	Cals	Fats	Choles	Carbs	Pros
Targets	*2000*	*80*	*300*	*250*	*90*
Totals					

If you <u>score</u>, you do <u>less</u> & <u>more</u>!

Quote of the Day

"The man who does not take pride in his own performance performs nothing in which to take pride."
Thomas J. Watson

Water

8	24	40	56	72	88	104	120
0	16	32	48	64	80	96	112	128

Breathing

AM		Noon		PM	

Goals

WEIGHT:	_____
EXERCISE:	_____
SCORE:	_____

"If it's to be, it's up to me!"

Power Performance

Daily Success Scorecard

Week: _____ 11 _____ Day: _____ 5 _____ Date: _____

Be Your Own Best Boss

Business Matters—*Nothing happens without engagement.*

    Primary ~ {40 Points} .... _____

    1. Money Makers   _____

    2. SAM Actions   _____

    Secondary ~ {20 Points}   .... _____

    1. R & D   _____

    2. Networking   _____

    Bizyness ~ {10 Points}   .... _____

    1. PATTs   _____

    2. G & A   _____

Nutrition—*Controlling our own destiny.*

    Calories ~ {7 Points} .... _____

    Nutraceuticals ~ {1 Point} .... _____

    Hydration ~ {2 Points} .... _____

Exercise—*Do it! Do it right! Do it right now!*

    Physical ~ {7 Points}   _____ _____

    Breathing ~ {3 Points} .... _____

Reading—*The man who reads is the man who leads.*   {5 Points} .... _____

    1. Spirituality ~ {2 Points}   _____

    2. Business ~ {2 Points}   _____

    3. Recreation ~ {1 Point}   _____

M.B.O.—*My future depends on many things, but mostly on me.*   {3 Points} .... _____

    1. Score ~ {1 Point}   _____

    2. Plan ~ {1 Point}   _____

    3. Save ~ {1 Point}   _____

Relationships—*"SMILE"*   {1 Point} .... _____

Personal Time—*"R & R 4me"*   {1 Point} .... _____

Selling = 4 to 5 hours a day

Total Daily Points ...   *"If not me, who?"*   .... _____

Target for the Day ...   *"If not now, when?"*   .... _____

My Can-Do Chant
"I can ... I will ... I'm good!"

Food Item	Cals	Fats	Choles	Carbs	Pros
Targets	*2000*	*80*	*300*	*250*	*90*
Totals					

If you <u>score</u>, you do <u>less</u> & <u>more!</u>

Quote of the Day

"The most effective way to do it, is to do it."
Amelia Earhart

Water

8	24	40	56	72	88	104	120
0	16	32	48	64	80	96	112	128

Breathing

AM		Noon		PM	

Goals

Weight:	_____
Exercise:	_____
Score:	_____

"If it's to be, it's up to me!"

Power Performance

Week: _____11_____   Day: _____6_____   Date: _____

Be Your Own Best Boss

Business Matters—*Nothing happens without engagement.*

    Primary ~ {40 Points} .... _____

    1. Money Makers   _____

    2. SAM Actions   _____

    Secondary ~ {20 Points}   .... _____

    1. R & D   _____

    2. Networking   _____

    Bizyness ~ {10 Points}   .... _____

    1. PATTs   _____

    2. G & A   _____

Nutrition—*Controlling our own destiny.*

    Calories ~ {7 Points}.. _____

    Nutraceuticals ~ {1 Point}.................................. _____

    Hydration ~ {2 Points} .... _____

Exercise—*Do it! Do it right! Do it right now!*

    Physical ~ {7 Points}   _____ _____

    Breathing ~ {3 Points} .... _____

Reading—*The man who reads is the man who leads.*   {5 Points} .... _____

    1. Spirituality ~ {2 Points}   _____

    2. Business ~ {2 Points}   _____

    3. Recreation ~ {1 Point}   _____

M.B.O.—*My future depends on many things, but mostly on me.*   {3 Points} .... _____

    1. Score ~ {1 Point}   _____

    2. Plan ~ {1 Point}   _____

    3. Save ~ {1 Point}   _____

Relationships—*"SMILE"*   {1 Point}......... _____

Personal Time—*"R & R 4me"*   {1 Point}......... _____

Selling = 4 to 5 hours a day

Total Daily Points ...   *"If not me, who?"*   .... _____

Target for the Day ...   *"If not now, when?*"   .... _____

My Can-Do Chant
"I can ... I will ... I'm good!"

FOOD ITEM	CALS	FATS	CHOLES	CARBS	PROS
Targets	*2000*	*80*	*300*	*250*	*90*
TOTALS					

If you <u>score</u>, you do <u>less</u> & <u>more</u>!

QUOTE OF THE DAY

"It's never too late to be what you might have been."
George Eliot

WATER

8	24	40	56	72	88	104	120
0	16	32	48	64	80	96	112	128

BREATHING

AM		Noon		PM	

GOALS

WEIGHT: _____
EXERCISE: _____
SCORE: _____

"If it's to be, it's up to me!"

Power Performance

Daily Success Scorecard

Week: ___11___   Day: ___7___   Date: _____

Be Your Own Best Boss

Business Matters—*Nothing happens without engagement.*

Primary ~ {40 Points} .... _____

1. Money Makers   _____

2. SAM Actions   _____

Secondary ~ {20 Points}   .... _____

1. R & D   _____

2. Networking   _____

Bizyness ~ {10 Points}   .... _____

1. PATTs   _____

2. G & A   _____

Nutrition—*Controlling our own destiny.*

Calories ~ {7 Points}... _____

Nutraceuticals ~ {1 Point}..................................... _____

Hydration ~ {2 Points} .... _____

Exercise—*Do it! Do it right! Do it right now!*

Physical ~ {7 Points}   _____ _____

Breathing ~ {3 Points} .... _____

Reading—*The man who reads is the man who leads.*   {5 Points} .... _____

1. Spirituality ~ {2 Points}   _____

2. Business ~ {2 Points}   _____

3. Recreation ~ {1 Point}   _____

M.B.O.—*My future depends on many things, but mostly on me.*   {3 Points} .... _____

1. Score ~ {1 Point}   _____

2. Plan ~ {1 Point}   _____

3. Save ~ {1 Point}   _____

Relationships—*"SMILE"*   {1 Point} .... _____

Personal Time—*"R & R 4me"*   {1 Point} .... _____

Selling = 4 to 5 hours a day

Total Daily Points ...   *"If not me, who?"*   .... _____

Target for the Day ...   *"If not now, when?*   .... _____

My Can-Do Chant
"I can … I will … I'm good!"

FOOD ITEM	CALS	FATS	CHOLES	CARBS	PROS
Targets	*2000*	*80*	*300*	*250*	*90*
TOTALS					

If you <u>score</u>, you do <u>less</u> & <u>more</u>!

QUOTE OF THE DAY

"No one can cheat you out of ultimate success but yourself."
Ralph Waldo Emerson

WATER

8	24	40	56	72	88	104	120
0	16	32	48	64	80	96	112	128

BREATHING

AM		Noon		PM	

GOALS

WEIGHT: _____
EXERCISE: _____
SCORE: _____

"If it's to be, it's up to me!"

Personal
Power Performance
Daily Success Scorecard

Week: _____ 12 _____   Day: _____ 1 _____   Date: _____

Be Your Own Best Boss

Business Matters—*Nothing happens without engagement.*

Primary ~ {40 Points} .... _____

  1. Money Makers   _____

  2. SAM Actions   _____

Secondary ~ {20 Points}   .... _____

  1. R & D   _____

  2. Networking   _____

Bizyness ~ {10 Points}   .... _____

  1. PATTs   _____

  2. G & A   _____

Nutrition—*Controlling our own destiny.*

Calories ~ {7 Points} .... _____

Nutraceuticals ~ {1 Point} .... _____

Hydration ~ {2 Points} .... _____

Exercise—*Do it! Do it right! Do it right now!*

Physical ~ {7 Points}   _____ _____

Breathing ~ {3 Points} .... _____

Reading—*The man who reads is the man who leads.*   {5 Points} .... _____

  1. Spirituality ~ {2 Points}   _____

  2. Business ~ {2 Points}   _____

  3. Recreation ~ {1 Point}   _____

M.B.O.—*My future depends on many things, but mostly on me.*   {3 Points} .... _____

  1. Score ~ {1 Point}   _____

  2. Plan ~ {1 Point}   _____

  3. Save ~ {1 Point}   _____

Relationships—*"SMILE"*   {1 Point} .... _____

Personal Time—*"R & R 4me"*   {1 Point} .... _____

Selling = 4 to 5 hours a day

Total Daily Points ...   *"If not me, who?"*   .... _____

Target for the Day ...   *"If not now, when?"*   .... _____

My Can-Do Chant
"I can ... I will ... I'm good!"

Food Item	Cals	Fats	Choles	Carbs	Pros
Targets	*2000*	*80*	*300*	*250*	*90*
Totals					

If you <u>score</u>, you do <u>less</u> & <u>more!</u>

Quote of the Day

"More men fail through lack of purpose than lack of talent."
Billy Sunday

Water

8		24		40		56		72		88		104		120	
0	16		32		48		64		80		96		112		128

Breathing

	AM			Noon			PM		

Goals

Weight:	_____
Exercise:	_____
Score:	_____

"If it's to be, it's up to me!"

156

Power Performance
Daily Success Scorecard

Week: ___12___   Day: ___2___   Date: _____

Be Your Own Best Boss

Business Matters—*Nothing happens without engagement.*

Primary ~ {40 Points} .... _____
1. Money Makers _____
2. SAM Actions _____
Secondary ~ {20 Points} .... _____
1. R & D _____
2. Networking _____
Bizyness ~ {10 Points} .... _____
1. PATTs _____
2. G & A _____

Nutrition—*Controlling our own destiny.*

Calories ~ {7 Points}... _____
Nutraceuticals ~ {1 Point}....................................... _____
Hydration ~ {2 Points} .... _____

Exercise—*Do it! Do it right! Do it right now!*

Physical ~ {7 Points} _____ _____
Breathing ~ {3 Points} .... _____

Reading—*The man who reads is the man who leads.*   {5 Points} .... _____
1. Spirituality ~ {2 Points} _____
2. Business ~ {2 Points} _____
3. Recreation ~ {1 Point} _____

M.B.O.—*My future depends on many things, but mostly on me.*   {3 Points} .... _____
1. Score ~ {1 Point} _____
2. Plan ~ {1 Point} _____
3. Save ~ {1 Point} _____

Relationships—*"SMILE"*   {1 Point} .... _____
Personal Time—*"R & R 4me"*   {1 Point} .... _____

Selling = 4 to 5 hours a day

Total Daily Points ...   *"If not me, who?"* .... _____
Target for the Day ...   *"If not now, when?* .... _____

MY CAN-DO CHANT
"I can ... I will ... I'm good!"

FOOD ITEM	CALS	FATS	CHOLES	CARBS	PROS
Targets	*2000*	*80*	*300*	*250*	*90*
TOTALS					

If you <u>score</u>, you do <u>less</u> & <u>more!</u>

QUOTE OF THE DAY
"The power of doing anything with quickness is always prized much by the possessor, and often without any attention to the imperfection of the performance."

Jane Austen

WATER

8	24	40	56	72	88	104	120
0	16	32	48	64	80	96	112	128

BREATHING

AM		Noon		PM	

GOALS

WEIGHT: _____
EXERCISE: _____
SCORE: _____

"If it's to be, it's up to me!"

158

Personal
Power Performance
Daily Success Scorecard

Week: _____ 12 _____   Day: _____ 3 _____   Date: _____

Be Your Own Best Boss

Business Matters—*Nothing happens without engagement.*

Primary ~ {40 Points} .... _____
1. Money Makers   _____
2. SAM Actions   _____
Secondary ~ {20 Points}   .... _____
1. R & D   _____
2. Networking   _____
Bizyness ~ {10 Points}   .... _____
1. PATTs   _____
2. G & A   _____

Nutrition—*Controlling our own destiny.*

Calories ~ {7 Points}.. _____
Nutraceuticals ~ {1 Point}................................. _____
Hydration ~ {2 Points} .... _____

Exercise—*Do it! Do it right! Do it right now!*

Physical ~ {7 Points}   _____ _____
Breathing ~ {3 Points} .... _____

Reading—*The man who reads is the man who leads.*   {5 Points} .... _____
1. Spirituality ~ {2 Points}   _____
2. Business ~ {2 Points}   _____
3. Recreation ~ {1 Point}   _____

M.B.O.—*My future depends on many things, but mostly on me.*   {3 Points} .... _____
1. Score ~ {1 Point}   _____
2. Plan ~ {1 Point}   _____
3. Save ~ {1 Point}   _____

Relationships—*"SMILE"*   {1 Point} .... _____
Personal Time—*"R & R 4me"*   {1 Point} .... _____

Selling = 4 to 5 hours a day

Total Daily Points ...   *"If not me, who?"*   .... _____
Target for the Day ...   *"If not now, when?*   .... _____

159

My Can-Do Chant
"I can ... I will ... I'm good!"

FOOD ITEM	CALS	FATS	CHOLES	CARBS	PROS
Targets	*2000*	*80*	*300*	*250*	*90*
TOTALS					

If you <u>score</u>, you do <u>less</u> & <u>more</u>!

QUOTE OF THE DAY

"Until you value yourself you will not value your time. Until you value your time, you will not do anything with it."
M. Scott Peck

WATER

8	24	40	56	72	88	104	120
0	16	32	48	64	80	96	112	128

BREATHING

AM		Noon		PM	

GOALS

WEIGHT: _____
EXERCISE: _____
SCORE: _____

"If it's to be, it's up to me!"

Power Performance
Daily Success Scorecard

Week: _____ 12 _____ Day: _____ 4 _____ Date: _____

Be Your Own Best Boss

Business Matters—*Nothing happens without engagement.*

Primary ~ {40 Points} .... _____
1. Money Makers   _____
2. SAM Actions   _____
Secondary ~ {20 Points}   .... _____
1. R & D   _____
2. Networking   _____
Bizyness ~ {10 Points}   .... _____
1. PATTs   _____
2. G & A   _____

Nutrition—*Controlling our own destiny.*

Calories ~ {7 Points}... _____
Nutraceuticals ~ {1 Point}.. _____
Hydration ~ {2 Points} .... _____

Exercise—*Do it! Do it right! Do it right now!*

Physical ~ {7 Points}   _____ _____
Breathing ~ {3 Points} .... _____

Reading—*The man who reads is the man who leads.*   {5 Points} .... _____
1. Spirituality ~ {2 Points}   _____
2. Business ~ {2 Points}   _____
3. Recreation ~ {1 Point}   _____

M.B.O.—*My future depends on many things, but mostly on me.*   {3 Points} .... _____
1. Score ~ {1 Point}   _____
2. Plan ~ {1 Point}   _____
3. Save ~ {1 Point}   _____

Relationships—*"SMILE"*   {1 Point} .... _____
Personal Time—*"R & R 4me"*   {1 Point} .... _____

Selling = 4 to 5 hours a day

Total Daily Points ...   *"If not me, who?"*   .... _____
Target for the Day ...   *"If not now, when?"* .... _____

My Can-Do Chant
"I can ... I will ... I'm good!"

FOOD ITEM	CALS	FATS	CHOLES	CARBS	PROS
Targets	*2000*	*80*	*300*	*250*	*90*
TOTALS					

If you <u>score</u>, you do <u>less</u> & <u>more!</u>

QUOTE OF THE DAY

"You only live once—but if you work it right, once is enough."
Joe E. Lewis

WATER

8	24	40	56	72	88	104	120
0	16	32	48	64	80	96	112	128

BREATHING

AM		Noon		PM	

GOALS

WEIGHT: _____
EXERCISE: _____
SCORE: _____

"If it's to be, it's up to me!"

Power Performance
Daily Success Scorecard

Week: ___12___ Day: ___5___ Date: _____

Be Your Own Best Boss

Business Matters—*Nothing happens without engagement.*

Primary ~ {40 Points} .... _____

  1. Money Makers   _____

  2. SAM Actions   _____

Secondary ~ {20 Points}   .... _____

  1. R & D   _____

  2. Networking   _____

Bizyness ~ {10 Points}   .... _____

  1. PATTs   _____

  2. G & A   _____

Nutrition—*Controlling our own destiny.*

Calories ~ {7 Points} .... _____

Nutraceuticals ~ {1 Point} .... _____

Hydration ~ {2 Points} .... _____

Exercise—*Do it! Do it right! Do it right now!*

Physical ~ {7 Points}   _____ _____

Breathing ~ {3 Points} .... _____

Reading—*The man who reads is the man who leads.*   {5 Points} .... _____

  1. Spirituality ~ {2 Points}   _____

  2. Business ~ {2 Points}   _____

  3. Recreation ~ {1 Point}   _____

M.B.O.—*My future depends on many things, but mostly on me.*   {3 Points} .... _____

  1. Score ~ {1 Point}   _____

  2. Plan ~ {1 Point}   _____

  3. Save ~ {1 Point}   _____

Relationships—*"SMILE"*   {1 Point} .... _____

Personal Time—*"R & R 4me"*   {1 Point} .... _____

Selling = 4 to 5 hours a day

Total Daily Points ... *"If not me, who?"* .... _____

Target for the Day ... *"If not now, when?* .... _____

163

My Can-Do Chant
"I can ... I will ... I'm good!"

Food Item	Cals	Fats	Choles	Carbs	Pros
Targets	*2000*	*80*	*300*	*250*	*90*
Totals					

If you <u>score</u>, you do <u>less</u> & <u>more</u>!

Quote of the Day
"The really happy people are those who have broken the chains of procrastination, those who find satisfaction in doing the job at hand. They're full of eagerness, zest, and productivity. You can be, too.
Norman Vincent Peale

Water

8		24		40		56		72		88		104		120	
0	16		32		48		64		80		96		112		128

Breathing

AM		Noon		PM	

Goals

Weight:	_____
Exercise:	_____
Score:	_____

"If it's to be, it's up to me!"

Personal
Power Performance
Daily Success Scorecard

Week: _____ 12 _____   Day: _____ 6 _____   Date: _____

Be Your Own Best Boss

__*Business Matters*__—*Nothing happens without engagement.*

    Primary ~ {40 Points} .... _____

    1. Money Makers   _____

    2. SAM Actions   _____

    Secondary ~ {20 Points}   .... _____

    1. R & D   _____

    2. Networking   _____

    Bizyness ~ {10 Points}   .... _____

    1. PATTs   _____

    2. G & A   _____

__*Nutrition*__—*Controlling our own destiny.*

    Calories ~ {7 Points} .... _____

    Nutraceuticals ~ {1 Point} .... _____

    Hydration ~ {2 Points} .... _____

__*Exercise*__—*Do it! Do it right! Do it right now!*

    Physical ~ {7 Points}   _____ _____

    Breathing ~ {3 Points} .... _____

__*Reading*__—*The man who reads is the man who leads.*   {5 Points} .... _____

    1. Spirituality ~ {2 Points}   _____

    2. Business ~ {2 Points}   _____

    3. Recreation ~ {1 Point}   _____

__*M.B.O.*__—*My future depends on many things, but mostly on me.*   {3 Points} ....

    1. Score ~ {1 Point}   _____

    2. Plan ~ {1 Point}   _____

    3. Save ~ {1 Point}   _____

__*Relationships*__—*"SMILE"*   {1 Point} .... _____

__*Personal Time*__—*"R & R 4me"*   {1 Point} .... _____

Selling = 4 to 5 hours a day

Total Daily Points ...   *"If not me, who?"*   .... _____

Target for the Day ...   *"If not now, when?"*   .... _____

165

My Can-Do Chant
"I can … I will … I'm good!"

FOOD ITEM	CALS	FATS	CHOLES	CARBS	PROS
Targets	*2000*	*80*	*300*	*250*	*90*
TOTALS					

If you <u>score</u>, you do <u>less</u> & <u>more</u>!

QUOTE OF THE DAY

"You're alive. Do something … Look. Listen. Choose. Act."
Barbara Hall

WATER

8	24	40	56	72	88	104	120
0	16	32	48	64	80	96	112	128

BREATHING

AM		Noon		PM	

GOALS

WEIGHT: _____
EXERCISE: _____
SCORE: _____

"If it's to be, it's up to me!"

Personal
Power Performance
Daily Success Scorecard

Week: _____12_____   Day: _____7_____   Date: _____

Be Your Own Best Boss

Business Matters—*Nothing happens without engagement.*

 Primary ~ {40 Points} .... _____
 1. Money Makers   _____
 2. SAM Actions   _____
 Secondary ~ {20 Points}   .... _____
 1. R & D   _____
 2. Networking   _____
 Bizyness ~ {10 Points}   .... _____
 1. PATTs   _____
 2. G & A   _____

Nutrition—*Controlling our own destiny.*

 Calories ~ {7 Points}... _____
 Nutraceuticals ~ {1 Point}...................................... _____
 Hydration ~ {2 Points} .... _____

Exercise—*Do it! Do it right! Do it right now!*

 Physical ~ {7 Points}   _____ _____
 Breathing ~ {3 Points} .... _____

Reading—*The man who reads is the man who leads.* {5 Points} .... _____
 1. Spirituality ~ {2 Points}   _____
 2. Business ~ {2 Points}   _____
 3. Recreation ~ {1 Point}   _____

M.B.O.—*My future depends on many things, but mostly on me.* {3 Points} .... _____
 1. Score ~ {1 Point}   _____
 2. Plan ~ {1 Point}   _____
 3. Save ~ {1 Point}   _____

Relationships—*"SMILE"*   {1 Point} .... _____
Personal Time—*"R & R 4me"*   {1 Point} .... _____

Selling = 4 to 5 hours a day

Total Daily Points ... *"If not me, who?"* .... _____
Target for the Day ... *"If not now, when?"* .... _____

FOOD ITEM	CALS	FATS	CHOLES	CARBS	PROS
Targets	*2000*	*80*	*300*	*250*	*90*
TOTALS					

If you <u>score</u>, you do <u>less</u> & <u>more</u>!

QUOTE OF THE DAY

"Some people make headlines while others make history."
Philip Elmer-DeWitt

WATER

8	24	40	56	72	88	104	120
0	16	32	48	64	80	96	112	128

BREATHING

AM		Noon		PM	

GOALS

WEIGHT: _____
EXERCISE: _____
SCORE: _____

"If it's to be, it's up to me!"

Power Performance

Daily Success Scorecard

Week: _____13_____   Day: _____1_____   Date: _____

Be Your Own Best Boss

Business Matters—*Nothing happens without engagement.*

    Primary ~ {40 Points} .... _____

    1. Money Makers   _____

    2. SAM Actions   _____

    Secondary ~ {20 Points}   .... _____

    1. R & D   _____

    2. Networking   _____

    Bizyness ~ {10 Points}   .... _____

    1. PATTs   _____

    2. G & A   _____

Nutrition—*Controlling our own destiny.*

    Calories ~ {7 Points}.. _____

    Nutraceuticals ~ {1 Point}.................................. _____

    Hydration ~ {2 Points} .... _____

Exercise—*Do it! Do it right! Do it right now!*

    Physical ~ {7 Points}   _____ _____

    Breathing ~ {3 Points} .... _____

Reading—*The man who reads is the man who leads.*   {5 Points} .... _____

    1. Spirituality ~ {2 Points}   _____

    2. Business ~ {2 Points}   _____

    3. Recreation ~ {1 Point}   _____

M.B.O.—*My future depends on many things, but mostly on me.* {3 Points} .... _____

    1. Score ~ {1 Point}   _____

    2. Plan ~ {1 Point}   _____

    3. Save ~ {1 Point}   _____

Relationships—*"SMILE"*   {1 Point} .... _____

Personal Time—*"R & R 4me"*   {1 Point} .... _____

Selling = 4 to 5 hours a day

Total Daily Points ...   *"If not me, who?"* .... _____

Target for the Day ...   *"If not now, when?* .... _____

My Can-Do Chant
"I can ... I will ... I'm good!"

Food Item	Cals	Fats	Choles	Carbs	Pros
Targets	*2000*	*80*	*300*	*250*	*90*
Totals					

If you <u>score</u>, you do <u>less</u> & <u>more</u>!

Quote of the Day

"The best way to break a bad habit is to drop it."
Leo Aikmain

Water

8	24	40	56	72	88	104	120
0	16	32	48	64	80	96	112	128

Breathing

AM		Noon		PM	

Goals

Weight:	_____
Exercise:	_____
Score:	_____

"If it's to be, it's up to me!"

Personal

Power Performance

Daily Success Scorecard

Week: ___13___   Day: ___2___   Date: _____

Be Your Own Best Boss

Business Matters—*Nothing happens without engagement.*

Primary ~ {40 Points} .... _____

1. Money Makers   _____

2. SAM Actions   _____

Secondary ~ {20 Points}   .... _____

1. R & D   _____

2. Networking   _____

Bizyness ~ {10 Points}   .... _____

1. PATTs   _____

2. G & A   _____

Nutrition—*Controlling our own destiny.*

Calories ~ {7 Points} .... _____

Nutraceuticals ~ {1 Point} .... _____

Hydration ~ {2 Points} .... _____

Exercise—*Do it! Do it right! Do it right now!*

Physical ~ {7 Points}   _____ _____

Breathing ~ {3 Points} .... _____

Reading—*The man who reads is the man who leads.*   {5 Points} .... _____

1. Spirituality ~ {2 Points}   _____

2. Business ~ {2 Points}   _____

3. Recreation ~ {1 Point}   _____

M.B.O.—*My future depends on many things, but mostly on me.*   {3 Points} .... _____

1. Score ~ {1 Point}   _____

2. Plan ~ {1 Point}   _____

3. Save ~ {1 Point}   _____

Relationships—*"SMILE"*   {1 Point} .... _____

Personal Time—*"R & R 4me"*   {1 Point} .... _____

Selling = 4 to 5 hours a day

Total Daily Points ...   *"If not me, who?"*   .... _____

Target for the Day ...   *"If not now, when?"*   .... _____

MY CAN-DO CHANT
"I can ... I will ... I'm good!"

FOOD ITEM	CALS	FATS	CHOLES	CARBS	PROS
Targets	*2000*	*80*	*300*	*250*	*90*
TOTALS					

If you <u>score</u>, you do <u>less</u> & <u>more</u>!

QUOTE OF THE DAY

"It's better to be prepared for an opportunity and not have one than to have an opportunity and not be prepared."
Whitney Young

WATER

8	24	40	56	72	88	104	120
0	16	32	48	64	80	96	112	128

BREATHING

AM		Noon		PM	

GOALS

WEIGHT: _____
EXERCISE: _____
SCORE: _____

"If it's to be, it's up to me!"

Personal
Power Performance
Daily Success Scorecard

Week: _____ 13 _____   Day: _____ 3 _____   Date: _____

Be Your Own Best Boss

Business Matters—*Nothing happens without engagement.*

    Primary ~ {40 Points} .... _____

    1. Money Makers   _____

    2. SAM Actions   _____

    Secondary ~ {20 Points}   .... _____

    1. R & D   _____

    2. Networking   _____

    Bizyness ~ {10 Points}   .... _____

    1. PATTs   _____

    2. G & A   _____

Nutrition—*Controlling our own destiny.*

    Calories ~ {7 Points}..................................... _____

    Nutraceuticals ~ {1 Point}............................. _____

    Hydration ~ {2 Points} .... _____

Exercise—*Do it! Do it right! Do it right now!*

    Physical ~ {7 Points}   _____ _____

    Breathing ~ {3 Points} .... _____

Reading—*The man who reads is the man who leads.*   {5 Points} .... _____

    1. Spirituality ~ {2 Points}   _____

    2. Business ~ {2 Points}   _____

    3. Recreation ~ {1 Point}   _____

M.B.O.—*My future depends on many things, but mostly on me.*   {3 Points} .... _____

    1. Score ~ {1 Point}   _____

    2. Plan ~ {1 Point}   _____

    3. Save ~ {1 Point}   _____

Relationships—*"SMILE"*   {1 Point} .... _____

Personal Time—*"R & R 4me"*   {1 Point} .... _____

Selling = 4 to 5 hours a day

Total Daily Points ...   *"If not me, who?"*   .... _____

Target for the Day ...   *"If not now, when?"*   .... _____

My Can-Do Chant
"I can ... I will ... I'm good!"

FOOD ITEM	CALS	FATS	CHOLES	CARBS	PROS
Targets	*2000*	*80*	*300*	*250*	*90*
TOTALS					

If you <u>score</u>, you do <u>less</u> & <u>more</u>!

QUOTE OF THE DAY

"Never mistake motion for action."
Ernest Hemingway

WATER

8	24	40	56	72	88	104	120
0	16	32	48	64	80	96	112	128

BREATHING

AM		Noon		PM	

GOALS

WEIGHT: _____
EXERCISE: _____
SCORE: _____

"If it's to be, it's up to me!"

174

Power Performance
Daily Success Scorecard

Week: _____13_____ Day: _____4_____ Date: _____

Be Your Own Best Boss

__Business Matters__—*Nothing happens without engagement.*

    Primary ~ {40 Points} .... _____

    1. Money Makers   _____

    2. SAM Actions   _____

    Secondary ~ {20 Points}   .... _____

    1. R & D   _____

    2. Networking   _____

    Bizyness ~ {10 Points}   .... _____

    1. PATTs   _____

    2. G & A   _____

__Nutrition__—*Controlling our own destiny.*

    Calories ~ {7 Points}.. _____

    Nutraceuticals ~ {1 Point}... _____

    Hydration ~ {2 Points} .... _____

__Exercise__—*Do it! Do it right! Do it right now!*

    Physical ~ {7 Points}   _____ _____

    Breathing ~ {3 Points} .... _____

__Reading__—*The man who reads is the man who leads.*   {5 Points} .... _____

    1. Spirituality ~ {2 Points}   _____

    2. Business ~ {2 Points}   _____

    3. Recreation ~ {1 Point}   _____

__M.B.O.__—*My future depends on many things, but mostly on me.*   {3 Points} .... _____

    1. Score ~ {1 Point}   _____

    2. Plan ~ {1 Point}   _____

    3. Save ~ {1 Point}   _____

__Relationships__—*"SMILE"*   {1 Point}......... _____

__Personal Time__—*"R & R 4me"*   {1 Point}......... _____

Selling = 4 to 5 hours a day

Total Daily Points ...   *"If not me, who?"*   .... _____

Target for the Day ...   *"If not now, when?*   .... _____

My Can-Do Chant
"I can ... I will ... I'm good!"

Food Item	Cals	Fats	Choles	Carbs	Pros
Targets	*2000*	*80*	*300*	*250*	*90*
Totals					

If you <u>score</u>, you do <u>less</u> & <u>more!</u>

Quote of the Day

"The distance isn't important; it is only the first step that is difficult."
Marie de Vichy-Chamrond

Water

8	24	40	56	72	88	104	120
0	16	32	48	64	80	96	112	128

Breathing

AM		Noon		PM	

Goals

Weight:	_____
Exercise:	_____
Score:	_____

"If it's to be, it's up to me!"

176

Personal
Power Performance
Daily Success Scorecard

Week: ___13___   Day: ___5___   Date: _____

Be Your Own Best Boss

Business Matters—*Nothing happens without engagement.*

Primary ~ {40 Points} .... _____
1. Money Makers   _____
2. SAM Actions   _____
Secondary ~ {20 Points}   .... _____
1. R & D   _____
2. Networking   _____
Bizyness ~ {10 Points}   .... _____
1. PATTs   _____
2. G & A   _____

Nutrition—*Controlling our own destiny.*

Calories ~ {7 Points}... _____
Nutraceuticals ~ {1 Point}..................................... _____
Hydration ~ {2 Points} .... _____

Exercise—*Do it! Do it right! Do it right now!*

Physical ~ {7 Points}   _____ _____
Breathing ~ {3 Points} .... _____

Reading—*The man who reads is the man who leads.*   {5 Points} .... _____
1. Spirituality ~ {2 Points}   _____
2. Business ~ {2 Points}   _____
3. Recreation ~ {1 Point}   _____

M.B.O.—*My future depends on many things, but mostly on me.*   {3 Points} .... _____
1. Score ~ {1 Point}   _____
2. Plan ~ {1 Point}   _____
3. Save ~ {1 Point}   _____

Relationships—*"SMILE"*   {1 Point} .... _____
Personal Time—*"R & R 4me"*   {1 Point} .... _____

Selling = 4 to 5 hours a day

Total Daily Points ...   *"If not me, who?"*   .... _____
Target for the Day ...   *"If not now, when?*   .... _____

MY CAN-DO CHANT
"I can ... I will ... I'm good!"

FOOD ITEM	CALS	FATS	CHOLES	CARBS	PROS
Targets	*2000*	*80*	*300*	*250*	*90*
TOTALS					

If you <u>score</u>, you do <u>less</u> & <u>more</u>!

QUOTE OF THE DAY

"Great minds have purposes, others have wishes."
Washington Irving

WATER

8	24	40	56	72	88	104	120
0	16	32	48	64	80	96	112	128

BREATHING

AM		Noon		PM	

GOALS

WEIGHT: _____
EXERCISE: _____
SCORE: _____

"If it's to be, it's up to me!"

Power Performance

Daily Success Scorecard

Week: _____ 13 _____   Day: _____ 6 _____   Date: _____

Be Your Own Best Boss

Business Matters—*Nothing happens without engagement.*

Primary ~ {40 Points} .... _____
1. Money Makers   _____
2. SAM Actions   _____

Secondary ~ {20 Points}   .... _____
1. R & D   _____
2. Networking   _____

Bizyness ~ {10 Points}   .... _____
1. PATTs   _____
2. G & A   _____

Nutrition—*Controlling our own destiny.*

Calories ~ {7 Points}...
Nutraceuticals ~ {1 Point}..................................... _____
Hydration ~ {2 Points} .... _____

Exercise—*Do it! Do it right! Do it right now!*

Physical ~ {7 Points}   _____
Breathing ~ {3 Points} .... _____

Reading—*The man who reads is the man who leads.*   {5 Points} .... _____
1. Spirituality ~ {2 Points}   _____
2. Business ~ {2 Points}   _____
3. Recreation ~ {1 Point}   _____

M.B.O.—*My future depends on many things, but mostly on me.*   {3 Points} .... _____
1. Score ~ {1 Point}   _____
2. Plan ~ {1 Point}   _____
3. Save ~ {1 Point}   _____

Relationships—*"SMILE"*   {1 Point}......... _____

Personal Time—*"R & R 4me"*   {1 Point}......... _____

Selling = 4 to 5 hours a day

Total Daily Points ...   *"If not me, who?"*   .... _____

Target for the Day ...   *"If not now, when?"*   .... _____

My Can-Do Chant
"I can ... I will ... I'm good!"

FOOD ITEM	CALS	FATS	CHOLES	CARBS	PROS
Targets	*2000*	*80*	*300*	*250*	*90*
TOTALS					

If you <u>score</u>, you do <u>less</u> & <u>more</u>!

QUOTE OF THE DAY

"If it is not right do not do it; if it is not true do not say it."
Marcus Aurelius

WATER

8		24		40		56		72		88		104		120	
0	16		32		48		64		80		96		112		128

BREATHING

AM		Noon		PM	

GOALS

WEIGHT: _____
EXERCISE: _____
SCORE: _____

"If it's to be, it's up to me!"

Power Performance

Daily Success Scorecard

Week: _____ 13 _____ Day: _____ 7 _____ Date: _____

Be Your Own Best Boss

Business Matters—*Nothing happens without engagement.*

 Primary ~ {40 Points} .... _____

 1. Money Makers   _____

 2. SAM Actions   _____

 Secondary ~ {20 Points}   .... _____

 1. R & D   _____

 2. Networking   _____

 Bizyness ~ {10 Points}   .... _____

 1. PATTs   _____

 2. G & A   _____

Nutrition—*Controlling our own destiny.*

 Calories ~ {7 Points}.. _____

 Nutraceuticals ~ {1 Point}... _____

 Hydration ~ {2 Points} .... _____

Exercise—*Do it! Do it right! Do it right now!*

 Physical ~ {7 Points}   _____ _____

 Breathing ~ {3 Points}.. _____

Reading—*The man who reads is the man who leads.* {5 Points} .... _____

 1. Spirituality ~ {2 Points}   _____

 2. Business ~ {2 Points}   _____

 3. Recreation ~ {1 Point}   _____

M.B.O.—*My future depends on many things, but mostly on me.* {3 Points} .... _____

 1. Score ~ {1 Point}   _____

 2. Plan ~ {1 Point}   _____

 3. Save ~ {1 Point}   _____

Relationships—*"SMILE"*   {1 Point}......... _____

Personal Time—*"R & R 4me"*   {1 Point}......... _____

Selling = 4 to 5 hours a day

Total Daily Points ... *"If not me, who?"* .... _____

Target for the Day ... *"If not now, when?* .... _____

My Can-Do Chant
"I can … I will … I'm good!"

Food Item	Cals	Fats	Choles	Carbs	Pros
Targets	*2000*	*80*	*300*	*250*	*90*
Totals					

If you <u>score</u>, you do <u>less</u> & <u>more</u>!

Quote of the Day

"I have the power to change and improve anything about me I want to."
Peter Biadasz

Water

8	24	40	56	72	88	104	120
0	16	32	48	64	80	96	112	128

Breathing

AM		Noon		PM	

Goals

Weight:	_____
Exercise:	_____
Score:	_____

"If it's to be, it's up to me!"

Congratulations!

Hallelujah, you have competed thirteen weeks of the Score-More Regimen. Now you know that this book is truly about changing behavior and instilling self-discipline. These two principles have made you a power-driven person. Did you know that changing behavior and sustaining that behavior change is more difficult than learning a new behavior? Furthermore, continued lengthy practice and ongoing follow-up are necessary to maintain your long-term changes and achieve powerful ongoing outcomes in your life.

We want your new behaviors to build you up and not tear you down. We want your current behaviors to take you toward and not away from your ultimate living-life goals. We want your behavior to be congruous with your personal values. Because when you behave right and proper, your internal feelings of self-worth increase. Thus, to help you stay focused, feel good about yourself, and grow as a power-driven individual, we strongly suggest that you continue on with the Score-More Regimen.

You can obtain more scorekeeping tally-tickets by placing an order at www.bepowerful.net. Please remember, learning theories emphasize that altering a complex pattern of behavior, like changing from a passive to a proactive lifestyle, normally require modifying many small behaviors that compose an overall complex system. Principles of behavior modification suggest that a complex pattern of behavior, such as weight management, exercise, and productivity, should be learned in small steps and tiny bites. Does this sound familiar? As you can see, this is the Score-More Regimen. Again, these incremental changes must be shaped over the long haul. Therefore, please don't stop now with the Score-

More Regimen. We don't want you to yo-yo your way through life. Thus, order your new supply of the Daily Success Scorecard's today. Don't let your powerful performance slip away. Congratulations on continuing your journey toward being a power-driven person, producing a more powerful living-life performance.

Peter Biadasz

Richard Possett

Conclusion

If you want to change your behavior, you must be committed. And, if you have just enthusiastically completed the first thirteen weeks of the Score-More Regimen, then you are a devoted individual. Your dedication has cultivated a power-driven personal culture of change. That is, to improve you through caretaking yourself, to redefine you by self-training, to reinvent yourself for a powerful performance in living life.

In the last thirteen weeks you have laid the groundwork for a new you. You have decided to create the individual center force for improved conduct and thinking, leading to better results. You have chosen to follow a time-tested course of action changing your behavior for a more hale and hearty lifestyle. You completed the process in small incremental acts. You did it one point at a time.

Using the Score-More Regimen, you determined to be accountable to yourself. It was your choice to choose. In the science of psychology, the concepts of internal locus of control and external locus of control are often used to talk about accountability. The latter group of people accounts their life events and circumstances to the external situation or to other people. These individuals play the "blame game" and live in a victim culture. The former describes those folks who account events and circumstances to themselves. They understand that true accountability and change is generated from within; it cannot be given from outside of oneself. This is you. You have chosen self-discipline over misbehavior, power over promiscuity.

However, to have a permanent internal locus of control takes time, energy, and effort. As you have proven, behavior can be changed; however, maintaining that change over time is more difficult. Therefore, we must stay the course for life fulfilling changes. We must not fall back and start using the 'short-cut' of "by-guess and by-golly." We must use the tally-ticket for accountability. According to the <u>Possett Proposition</u>, if you don't know, then you are out of control. And without the tally, you don't know the score. Maintaining the perpetual self-discipline of score-keeping is the positive personal action that ensures a power-driven performance in life. And, scoring is the best way; no, the only way, to maintain control over you and what you do. This is true because if you score, you do less and more!

☑ *LESS*	☑ *MORE*
• Bizyness	• Business
• Bingeing	• Nutritious eating
• Woolgathering	• Introspection
• Forlorn	• Relationships
• Fallowness	• Life-long learning
• Sloth	• Dynamism
• Stress	• Confidence
• Fatigue	• Energy
• Illness	• Wellness

Now, let's have a toast to health, wealth, and wisdom. It is all within your personal power. It can be done if you plan your work and work your plan. Each and every day, be totally aware of your matters, mind, body, and spirit. Focus on the business of getting business and not just bizyness. Be frugal, but not cheap. Both spend and save. Do your power breathing exercises three times each day. Practice good posture. Daily, stretch your mind and muscles. Eat, drink, and be merry, more and less. Get and stay fit, mentally, physically, and spiritually. Score for less and more. Use the tally-ticket. Recognize that little daily changes cascade into a changed life. Thus, each of us will live a power-driven life and grow until we die. And this is true wisdom. Let's grasp wisdom by not repeating our mistakes. We will err and our errors are our failures. Then, let us fail, but let us learn from them. Let us teach by guidance and example throughout our lives and pass forward our successes. Let us properly care-take ourselves with integrated fitness. Through this we generate a more powerful living-life performance. We become a real power-driven person. We emerge a powerful performer.

Oh! What about Ralphie? He is looking good, feeling much better, and doing real well. He lost forty-four pounds in just over fifteen months. His scale weight is one hundred and seventy-four. Of course, he has become a devoted enthusiast of the Score-More Regimen He exercises as scheduled, maintains his weight management discipline, reads regularly, and pays more attention to relationships. In business matters, he avoids bizyness and concentrates on money makers. Ralphie adheres to the Power-Performers, drinks a lot of water, watches his posture, systematically engages in power breathing, takes glyconutrients as a dietary supplement, plays more, and is soulfully spiritual.

Glossary

Bizyness: suggests action in some project, assignment, task, and/or to-do having very little or no value-added to the mission of the business.

CALS: this means calories.

CARBS: this means carbohydrates.

CHOLES: this means cholesterol.

FUBAR: meaning *fouled up beyond all recognition*. A stressful, anxious, agitated, and apprehensive state of affairs caused by mistake, misfeasance, confusion, wrongdoing, depression, and/or fear.

G & A: stands for *general and administrative* matters.

IF: refers to integrated fitness of a person's mind, body, and spirit necessary for comprehensive wellness.

If-onlys: to have a longing for something; want; desire; crave. If only I had this or that, wouldn't things be better.

Jogawalkie: an exercise routine where one walks downhill and jogs uphill.

M.B.O: relates to the business planning and control process of *management by objectives*.

Money Makers: activity in the enterprise that clearly and concisely produces revenue and cash flow.

Ne Fas: denotes the permission to proclaim a day off from dieting.

Networking: the state of fellowship having common personal and professional interests and purposes. In networking, we create personal friendships and professional relationships of mutual interest and for bilateral benefit. The purpose of networking is to develop symbiotic relationships producing synergistic rewards.

Nutraceuticals: generally accepted dietary supplements taken daily.

Paramount Virtues: pre-eminent precepts of moral excellence.

- ◆ Do worship only the supreme reality
- ◆ Don't desire what belongs to another
- ◆ Do be faithful in totality
- ◆ Don't idolize any thing whatever
- ◆ Do have fidelity to family and community
- ◆ Don't murder, thieve, curse, or foreswear
- ◆ Do honor your forebears
- ◆ Don't work or rest without purpose
- ◆ Do respect others, yourself, and thy partner
- ◆ Don't squander your living life and soul

PATTs: signifies *projects, assignments, tasks, and to-does.*

PROS: this means proteins.

R & D: refers to *research and development* doings; the skunk works.

SAM: this is the *sales and marketing* function of the enterprise.

Tally-ticket: the Score-More Regimen recordkeeping sheet, i.e., Daily Success Scorecard.

Vanposetski: the pseudonym for the author, Richard Possett.

Possett's Power-Performers

1. *Cellular~Power* speaks to the brain and how it matters for a healthy life.

2. *Fund~Power* has to do with our moneyed possessions and the stewardship of them.

3. *Hydro~Power* is the source of stamina that is derived from H_2O.

4. *Hypo~Power* is that real but vague superhuman potency of mind over matter.

5. *Mine~Power* is the Goal Mine of forethought, preparing, and planning.

6. *Moto~Power* is the dynamic might manifested by physical exercise.

7. *Nuke~Power* is the functioning anatomical vitality in our physique.

8. *Nutra~Power* is the personal energy that comes from proper dietary supplements.

9. *Nutri~Power* is the cornucopia of strength that comes from nutritious food.

10. *Pay~Power* is our salary, commission, wage, bonus, or other compensation.

11. *People~Power* is the quality and state of our attached kinships.

12. *Play~Power* is our ability to engage in recreation and have some fun in life.

13. *Psycho~Power* relates to our personal sanity and mental fitness.

14. *Soulur~Power* is the true essence and substance of our being. It is our strong spirituality.

15. *Wind~Power* is the tour de force that power breathing brings to our overall well-being.

છ્ર ૐ

Possett's Powerful Pithy Pointers

1. A good life well lived matters. Have a powerful living-life performance.

2. Focus on business and not bizyness. The results are rewarding.

3. Stop thinking of food as a reward or meals as entertainment.

4. Most meals are for health and sustenance, nothing more.

5. Have simple but clear, definite, time bound, and factual goals.

6. Come up with REALISTIC objectives and strategies.

7. Plan. Plan. Plan.

8. In your plan, account for special times (birthdays, holidays, PTO days, etc.) and "FUBAR" situations because "stuff" still happens.

9. Make your plan the priority. There will be sacrifices in fun, time, and money. No pain—no gain!

10. Don't set yourself up for failure. Go slow but have some fun. Please remember the *Ne Fas* days.

11. Exercise. Exercise. Exercise.

12. Eat a healthy mix of foods (roughly one-third protein, one-third fats, and one-third carbs).

13. Record everything you do on the daily tally-ticket, even on off days. Yes, write it down on the scorecard.

14. Chart your progress daily, weekly, monthly, and annually. Track your scale weight, clothing size, notches on the belt, and exercise time and distance, for the little successes. They get bigger.

15. Drink H_2O. Drink H_2O. Drink H_2O.

16. Eat good and eat well. Have a healthy relationship with food that has defined boundaries. Realize who is master and slave.

17. Give yourself breaks, but don't go overboard. Don't erase a lot of good hard work.

18. Tell yourself over and over that without exercise, a lot of your work may be a waste. Waste not—want not!

19. Throw out any weekend junk food on Sunday night. Quickly get to the point where you stop buying weekend junk food.

20. Power Breathe. Power Breathe. Power Breathe.

21. Be mindful of everything you are eating, both food and serving size.

22. Savor your entertainment meals. Food will never taste better. Again, mindfulness and moderation.

23. Pass the dessert please, but wait thirty (30) minutes first. It takes that long for your stomach to tell the brain that it is full.

24. Once you go down a clothing size, get rid of the bigger items immediately. Don't give yourself an excuse, an out.

25. Read. Read. Read.

26. Provide for an adequate grocery budget. Eating well can be expensive.

27. Don't ever go to the store hungry. Shame on you if you do.

28. Remind yourself that the point of your efforts is not for fun, but health and wellness. Remember it really does get easier.

29. Take good dietary supplements every day.

30. Stretch before you exercise. Don't overdo! If you do, think of all the recovery time during which you will not be burning calories.

31. Decide on a good exercise plan with professional help.

32. Relate. Relate. Relate.

33. Don't be a zealot. Mindfulness and moderation in all things.

34. Graze throughout the day. Eating something small every two (2) hours or so keeps your metabolism working well.

35. If you wait until you are hungry, you will most likely overeat.

36. Never skip breakfast. Start the day the right way.

37. Score for less and more because success is one point at a time.

38. Work hard at your power performance program, BUT have some fun along the way.

CR SO

Appendix III

Possett's Powerful Pithy Pointers *TOO*

<u>*Good foods eaten regularly during the week*</u>

1. Kashi Glycemic Control Bars

2. Yoplait Light Yogurt

3. Buddig Turkey or Chicken

4. String Cheese

5. Beef or Turkey Jerky

6. Boiled Egg Whites

7. Canned Salmon or Tuna

8. Smoked Salmon or Tuna

9. Trader Joe's Seafood Medley

10. Steak and Chicken Tenderloins

11. Kashi Heart Smart Cereal

12. Nature Valley Chewey Granola Bars

13. Bear Naked Peak Protein Granola

14. Soy and Veggie Crisps

15. Apples, Cherries, Bananas, Blueberries, and Melons

16. Trader Joe's Chicken Chipotle Sausage

17. Sauerkraut, Green Beans, Spinach, and Bean Sprouts

18. Banana Peppers

19. Salad, Vegetables, and Fruits

20. Trader Joe's Best Trek Mix Ever

21. Trader Joe's Turkey Meat Balls

22. Red and White Wine

23. Crystal and Minute Maid Lite

24. Cedarlane Cous Veggie Wrap

25. Low Fat Nilla Wafers

26. Haagen Daz (yes, the real stuff)

27. Belgian Chocolate with Almonds

28. Trader Joe's Chocolate Wafer Cookies

29. Cheerios, Rice Krispies, and Wheaties

30. You discover the cornucopia. It is there waiting for you in the grocery store if you look.

ℰᎦ ᏟᏒ

About the Authors

Peter Biadasz (pronounced *bee-ahd-ish*) has been in numerous leadership positions in many groups and organizations since junior high school. As a leader, Peter not only shares his vision for each organization and the office that he holds, but carefully leads the members to fulfill the vision in a manner that creates win/win scenarios that are in the best interest of the organization. Both personally and professionally, Peter has always attempted to teach by word and example a powerfully balanced lifestyle. Additionally, Peter has been known to utilize his professional trumpet talent to liven up speaking engagements.

Peter is a graduate of Florida State University. His passion for and expertise in the area of leadership has aided many over the years. Leadership and the skills required to become a great leader are essential in reaching the next level of success. Experience has shown that the people and groups working with Peter have an increase in the quality of leadership skills. Furthermore, an excitement for the topics at hand, as never before seen, emerges as those involved transform into distinguished and mature leaders.

The father of an incredible son and precious daughter, Peter is also the author of *MORE LEADS: The Complete Handbook for TIPS Groups, Leads Groups, and Networking Groups* and co-author of the Power Series, of which this book is a part. Please visit with Peter at www.getmoreleads.net or www.bepowerful.net.

Richard Possett is a forty-five year experienced entrepreneur and seasoned executive from the international financial and insurance services industries. Richard was born and raised in Grand Rapids, Michigan. He lived and worked for five years in Los Angeles, California, before moving to Mid-America where he and his family have resided for the last eighteen years.

Richard graduated from Western Michigan University with a BBA degree, earning a major in accountancy. He is a CPA, small business owner, accredited mortgage loan originator, financialist, and past SEC-registered securities representative and licensed insurance agent.

Richard is a former international rugby player. He served in the United States Army during the Vietnam War. He has been married to his spouse, best friend, and mate, Marilyn, for more than forty-one wonderful years. The couple has three awesome adult children, three beautiful young grandchildren, and a great son-in-law. Richard's interests include reading, writing, and walking with his wife and their two golden retrievers, Jordie and Doolie.

Richard is an award-winning author. For a complete catalogue of his literary works, visit www.bepossettive.com. To personally contact Richard, please feel free to email him at richard@bepossitive.com. He would love to hear from everyone.

Index of Individuals Quoted

Index of Topics Quoted

Note: Many quotes may fit into more than one category.

The  Books

The 'Power Series' books mean what they say and say what they mean. They are powerful and contain the dynamism to make you a power-driven person. The books are about the reader learning how to effectively acquire and utilize productive power in all facets of their life: personal and professional, at home, work, and play. The books are not concerned with dominion, authority, and control. These books are about health, wealth, and happiness. The 'Power Series' books provide the principles and practices that can produce a lifestyle full of wellness and success.

There are many-many elements that make a powerful person. Such essentials as relationships, leadership, networking, teaching, listening, learning, spirituality, character, and health make a short and incomplete list. The material and information in the power-books speak to what it takes to be powerful in living life. The aforementioned areas are part and parcel of what it takes to be a powerful person. The syllabus could go on ad infinitum. Currently, 'Power Series' book titles include the following:

Powerful People Have Powerful Character
Powerful People Overcome Powerful Failures
Powerful People Play Powerful Golf
Powerful People Have Powerful Health
Powerful People Are Powerful I.T. Professionals
Powerful People Are Powerful Leaders
Powerful People Are Powerful Learners

Powerful People Are Powerful Listeners
Powerful People Have Powerful Meekness
Powerful People Have Powerful Money
Powerful People Are Powerful Networkers
Powerful People Have Powerful Personalities
Powerful People Have Powerful Relationships
Powerful People Are Powerful Risk Managers
Powerful People Are Powerful Teachers

More Power Titles to Be Released Next Year

To learn more about the 'Power Series' as well as to order additional books, please visit www.bepowerful.net. The 'Power Series' books are the production of Peter Biadasz and Richard Possett. You can learn more about the producers in the "About the Authors" section of the book you are now holding in your hands.

A Chuncated Approach

The Chuncated Learning System, or *CLS*, is an effective way of acquiring knowledge and information for positive growth and change in your personal and professional life. It is the method of learning used in the 'Power Series' books. *CLS* can be a highly cogent technique for changing personality style gradually by learning and applying facts and scholarship incrementally.

A big part of *CLS* is the small. This is because the method takes a body of work and breaks it down into little fun parts. *CLS* is effective because it teaches a big concept in small daily bite sizes. It is a process we call "chunking." The approach takes a huge hunk of knowledge and breaks it down into wee nuggets for easier learning. It is very much like baby steps. That is, scholarship in tiny short strides.

In each 'Power Series' book, there are exercises to be completed and/or reviewed over a period of one year. These tasks are assigned as homework, to be done daily in a fun, fast, and easy way. Empirically, we have come to know that the earthborn learn best from consistent daily study and practice. It reframes and reinforces. Then, over many weeks, a new awareness of oneself emerges, shaping a powerfully enhanced personality style.

With each simple exercise thoroughly and thoughtfully completed, the user of a 'Power Series' book receives a small reward, a little flash of accomplishment. It is the ecstatic titillation of self-admiration; the euphoric sense of self-confidence. This sensation is the wonderfully good feeling of a job well done. And each shot of "feel good" is like a small reward reinforcing a newly learned concept. By gradually shaping, hunk-by-chunk, our thoughts and actions, *CLS* strongly influences an improved personality style having the power of presence and poise.

CLS was adopted for the 'Power Series' books because of its simple and straightforward approach to learning. In the hurly-burly of modern society, it is often difficult, as an adult, to continue one's education. The constraints of work and family responsibilities can frequently retard our personal growth and capability to improve the self. *CLS*, with its "chunking" process, helps to mitigate these factors. Thus, by simply setting aside a very small part of your busy day and focusing on learning in bite sizes, you can grow more powerful with your newly applied knowledge, one day at a time.

978-0-595-41844-2
0-595-41844-9

www.ingramcontent.com/pod-product-compliance
Lightning Source LLC
Chambersburg PA
CBHW051228050326
40689CB00007B/846